SECRETS FROM BEYOND THE PYRAMIDS

Geof Gray-Cobb

Parker Publishing Company
West Nyack, New York

© 1979, *by*

PARKER PUBLISHING COMPANY, INC.

West Nyack, N.Y.

All rights reserved. No part of this book may be reproduced in any form or by any means, without permission in writing from the publisher.

This book is a reference work based on research by the author. The opinions expressed herein are not necessarily those of or endorsed by the Publisher.

Library of Congress Cataloging in Publication Data

Gray-Cobb, Geof
    Secrets from beyond the pyramids.

    1. Success.   2. Occult sciences.   3. Pyramids–
Miscellanea.   I. Title.
BJ1611.2.G73   131'.32   79-16415
ISBN 0-13-797886-3

Printed in the United States of America

Dedication:

To the Founders and Builders of the Astral City, without whose discipline and dedication I might never have been privileged to point the Way.

Previous books by Geof Gray-Cobb:

The Miracle of New Avatar Power
Amazing Secrets of New Avatar Power

Why This Book
Will Fulfill Every Need

My most sincere greetings to you, a special person. A person for whom this book was especially written: someone who is nursing a dream—perhaps some call it a hopeless dream—of health, wealth, happiness, peace and companionship.

My warmest welcome to you as you read these opening words, because I wrote them for *you*. Between us now exists a bond, welded by destiny. The simple fact that my words are now in your hands *proves* the first step of a miraculous transformation has already taken place.

You may think chance alone put this book in your hands, but I ask you to consider a different idea. I knew when I set out to type the first draft of this book that fate would place it unerringly in the hands of the people who need it most.

You, therefore, are one of those people. And why do you need this book? Stay with me for a few more pages and I'll tell you.

BEYOND PYRAMID POWER

Have you heard about Pyramid Power, that mystic energy which researchers have found connected with all pyramids?

Whether we look at the Great Pyramids in Egypt, or model pyramids made in your own home, wonderful things happen in and around them. Investigators have discovered that the pyramid shape conjures up forms of energy which affect objects and change natural laws, bringing sensational and unexplainable happenings.

Whether or not you've heard of Pyramid Power is unimportant. This book takes you far above Pyramid Power into a new discovery which you can simply and easily use, transforming your personal life into incredible shapes of satisfaction, riches and contentment.

As we proceed together through this book we'll be looking at and creating personal miracle-working a quantum leap beyond yesterday's Pyramid Power. Simply stated, we will work together, safely and easily, changing your most secret dreams into stupendous reality.

I shall be beside you every step of the way, showing you what to do and how to apply the simple techniques which tune you in to a mighty Tide of Cosmic Power, a Tide I have named *New Psychic Energy Power*. You will also notice me calling this Psychic Pyramidic Power, Cosmic Energy, Pyramid Energy, Pyramid Power—they all mean exactly the same thing, identifying this life-transforming energy flow.

I have a very specific reason for so confidently stating that claim. Right at the beginning I greeted you as someone special, and that's precisely true.

You *are* special, because you're reading this book. The first step in your use of *New Psychic Energy Power* to transform your life is already a fact. The truth that you're reading this book is positive proof of that: fate arranged it thus, using *New Psychic Energy Power* to accomplish it.

WHY THIS BOOK WILL FULFILL EVERY NEED

The whole of this manuscript is being composed with the help of *New Psychic Energy Power*. I'm putting the words in order and attending to all the details of making sure the pages are numbered and the publisher gets the typed pages on time.

But *behind*, above and beyond that visible effort is an incredible, invisible reservoir of energy which is helping things along, making everything go right, ensuring that nothing can stand in the way of this vital message reaching you.

I've applied one of the techniques I discovered to make absolutely certain of this. And it *has* happened, just as I knew it would: you and I are united by *New Psychic Energy Power* to move you unerringly into new, exciting and satisfying conditions which you may have been awaiting throughout your life so far, just as did Dexter D. in the case history from my files which follows.

"EVERYTHING CAME UP ROSES" FOR PREVIOUS LOSER DEXTER D.

In one of the sumptuous homes on Hollywood's Sunset Boulevard lives a mystery man. Few people know where he came from, or how he acquired vast wealth. You are about to learn his story—or as much of it as he will permit me to tell you.

The trappings of big money surround his life. His antique and contemporary furnishings were all imported at great expense from Europe. His weekly "walking-around money" would keep the average family adequately sheltered and nourished for a full year. His 17 personal vehicles range from a custom-built golfcart with bar and TV, to a Rolls Royce which was originally built for an oil sheik. Word has it that when the sheik saw the bill for the option-laden package of gold-plated automobile he said he could not afford the price. Our man on Sunset Boulevard could, and did!

WHY THIS BOOK WILL FULFILL EVERY NEED

You'll rarely find him in Hollywood. He's often away in the jet-spots of the globe with his loving and beautiful showgirl wife and their two children.

Or if they're not lazing around in Cannes, the Bahamas, Australian beaches, Las Vegas or some other high life area, you might find them quietly savoring life in their luxurious chalet high in the Swiss Alps. And if they're not there, you might see if they're staying at one of the 23 luxury hotels this man owns worldwide.

He's known simply as "Mr. D." to the obedient staff of employees whose sole job is to see that he's as happy, contented, unharried and healthy as dedicated service can make him.

I was lucky enough to meet him in the plush offices of a large movie production organization near Wilshire Boulevard, Los Angeles. Mr. D. had decided he'd use some of his surplus cash to make a movie and he was enjoying himself hugely.

He greeted me like a long-lost friend—which you might say was almost true: I knew of Mr. D. when he was simply Dexter D., a hopeless and despairing unemployed laborer from Chicago.

Dexter had slipped across the border into Canada to see if it was any easier to keep body and soul together in Toronto than it had been in his home city.

"It most decidedly was not," he says. "Life went from bad to worse to abominable."

Because of his current high profile, Mr. D. has asked me not to list the specific degradations he experienced in two years which plumbed the depths of atrocious misery for him.

"I guess the turning point came when, out of try-anything-once desperation, I picked up a used copy of a psychic self-help book," Mr. D. said. "The guaranteed miracles offered a slim ray of hope. Yet I could not make it work. Despite chanting, prayer, affirmations, positive thinking and applying all the rest of the instructions, nothing good happened to me.

WHY THIS BOOK WILL FULFILL EVERY NEED 11

"I used my last few cents to write a bitter letter to the author of the book to say it was a rip-off."

Fate stepped in at that point. As occasionally happens in a large organization, Dexter's letter was misfiled at the publisher's offices. Instead of being mailed to the correct author, his letter was sent to me along with the rest of the packages of forwarded mail which reach me two or three times each week, year round.

This book was in draft form, so I sent Dexter a few suggestions which basically suggested how he might stop battling against destiny and instead flow with Cosmic Tides.

That early data is now updated, streamlined and improved in the pages of this book you're holding.

"The way to wealth opened up like magic," Dexter said. "Within two months I was working, with money in the bank. Inside six months I was my own boss. From there it was an easy ride to sheer opulence. Doors opened automatically, windfalls cascaded into my lap, I always seemed to be in the right place at exactly the right time. Dame Fortune was smiling on me fit to split her face—and she has never ceased beaming on me.

"I would prefer not to go into details because I value my privacy. Enough people want to know the secret of my success without my being asked to instruct them in the gentle art of using *New Psychic Energy Power*.

"We should merely say everything came up roses for me!"

You can emulate Dexter (which is not the name he now uses, by the way). Soaring from misery to ecstasy is just a few simple steps away, using a new improved version of the method I originally suggested to poor Dexter D. who promptly soared to an apex of everything that is best in life.

GAIN YOUR RIGHTFUL REWARDS WITH NEW PSYCHIC ENERGY POWER

To repeat: this book was *destined* to reach you, and the

WHY THIS BOOK WILL FULFILL EVERY NEED

fact that it has done so shows we're well on the way to helping you reap the rewards which are your birthright, as a fully accredited member of the human race, a God-created intelligence in this Universe.

You'll read more of this as we proceed. You'll see how ordinary people just like yourself (and others in even deeper trouble) found their way quickly and easily out of turmoil, to become the peaceful, ongoing and happy beings Nature intended them to be.

This Universe works in a sacred harmony of rhythms and cycles. Astronomers, statisticians, astrologers, biorhythm users and many other disciplines recognize and use such cycles. The stars swing through space, grouped in galaxies; planets swim around their suns in well-defined paths; and on the inhabited planets, plants and animals grow in the midst of the ebb and flow of energies that govern the tides of existence.

Within that divine pattern only one single thing causes pain, turmoil and confusion. Anything that steps out of line, deliberately or accidentally, with the supreme swings of Natural Energies becomes opposed to the tidal cycles of Nature.

Then, just as swimming against any tide needs extra effort, whoever or whatever is out of tune with the natural pattern meets delays, chaos, exhaustion, pain and lack of progress.

Luckily, there's a simple cure: realignment with Natural Energies makes the pain recede, and progress begins again.

See where I'm taking you with my reasoning? What I'm saying is that if you're not as successful, happy, peaceful and harmonious as Nature and God intended you to be, then you must be struggling against one or other of the natural tides of Nature.

So all you need to do to achieve true happiness and harmony is to tune yourself in to Cosmic Energies, and automatically you'll see life changes which place you on a happy path to fulfillment.

WHY THIS BOOK WILL FULFILL EVERY NEED

Almost inevitably your next question will be: "How do I know which tide I'm battling against?"

And the answer is, "You do not necessarily need to find out. *New Psychic Energy Power* will do the identification and life-changing *for* you."

That's precisely what you, this book and I are doing together. I've found *New Psychic Energy Power* to be one of the greatest life-manipulating energies around. No doubt there are other hidden energies still awaiting discovery in this Age of Aquarius, but right now *New Psychic Energy Power* is the one for *you* to use. Destiny has proven that: into the Cosmic Flow of Akashic Happenings I deliberately requested that *New Psychic Energy Power* methods should reach those people who would gain most benefit from them—people such as you, or Betty S. whose delightful life transformation is described next.

BETTY S. SOARED FROM MISERY TO TOTAL CONTENTMENT

"One thing I did not have a while ago was the worst credit rating in the world," Betty S. writes. "By no means: I had no credit rating at all! I was so far in over my head that even if I'd found a good job and worked 100 hours a week I would still have been paying off debts at the age of 92.

"So how come I'm so happy now, with cash to spare and everything that makes life worth living? Let me tell you what happened to me in a few short months.

"I was the eldest of seven children born on a farm in the Ozarks. Mom and Pop were good people, grindingly poor, who worked from sun-up to dark, never making enough to go round.

"I grew up thinking that was the way it should be for the likes of us, until I met this smooth traveling man. He whisked me off to Nevada with empty promises, then left me cold after he'd knocked me up.

14   *WHY THIS BOOK WILL FULFILL EVERY NEED*

"I got hit by a hit-and-run driver and broke my hip, lost the baby and almost died. Downhill all the way from there. Standing was agony so being a waitress was out. I'd had precious little schooling so office jobs were closed to me.

"I was so rundown and shattered I took to booze, shoplifting and petty crime.

"Even that might have been bearable, but I never found a true friend down there. Always achingly alone, never a smile from a familiar face, on the run from various cities where the law wanted me.

"I changed my name and tried to make a fresh start. That failed. All I put together was debts to go with my misery and loneliness.

"I was working part-time as a cleaner at a rundown motel for starvation wages when I came across a paperback book on Pyramid Power a guest had left behind. Figured a little reading would cost nothing so I spent long hours stumbling through it.

"But no sooner had I gotten the idea of pyramids into my head than things started to happen.

"First up was a new job. Still cleaning at a motel, but at better wages at a higher class establishment. That's where I met Fred, a guest who was passing through.

"By that time, although still in deep trouble moneywise, I'd managed to buy a few new clothes and afford a little make-up. And believe me, even those little things seemed like the most incredible luxuries after the dregs I'd wallowed in.

"Fred and I hit it off. We married, and his small trucking business boomed when I helped with the paperwork. We started a family, bought a good home, and added those touches of money I never thought I'd ever see.

"No, we're not part of the filthy rich. Very comfortable though, with no worries. With Fred's TLC you can mark me down as having gone from utter misery to total contentment."

In her own words, you have just read the amazing transformation that occurred for Betty S. after merely touching on the subject of pyramids and reading about their powers.

WHY THIS BOOK WILL FULFILL EVERY NEED

15

This is an unusual case which might not happen for everybody. But consider what *you* can do with the techniques in this book: pyramid methods distilled and refined so that you're in line to double or treble the bounty and luck which came Betty's way so easily.

NEW PSYCHIC ENERGY POWER BRINGS PERSONAL MIRACLES

By now you've read about two people who experienced their own personal miracles. As you'll know if you've read any of my other books, my firm opinion is that *reading* about people is fine and dandy, as it shows you what can be done and gives you targets at which to aim.

But I also know you want these marvelous things to happen to you, because reading about another person's miracles is very much like being a starving person peering into a warm restaurant watching other people enjoying fine fare.

Worry not: along with the case histories, which incidentally frequently contain valuable tips and wrinkles on exactly how to apply these techniques, we're coming to the exact and precise methods of creating personal miracles for you. It's almost as easy as reading about other people's, but infinitely more rewarding.

As I advise you on the "how" of it, step by simple step, in the following pages you'll understand how Pyramid Energies can be applied to your life.

You'll see how nature has equipped you with three pyramid tools which are part of your physical body, and from which you can draw an unending stream of vital energy to sweep away cares and replace them with happiness, to literally carry you to the most glittering peak of perfection you can imagine.

Together we'll travel the four faces of a pyramid, seeing how *New Psychic Energy Power* operates for you in various ways, to bring riches, love, protection and health.

16 *WHY THIS BOOK WILL FULFILL EVERY NEED*

We'll actually construct a *New Psychic Energy Generator* as a tangible and visible source of your miracle-working energy.

I'll show you mystic symbols which have come from the Egyptian pyramids, such as the *Golden Square of Prithivi* which creates money, and the *Glacial Ring-Pass-Not* which ensures that its user never again runs up a debt he or she cannot handle.

The *Blue Circle of Vayu*, the *Scarlet Triangle of Tejas*, the *Sunshine Protection Routine*, the *Silver Crescent of Apas*, the *Western Water Technique* ... all of those and many more I'll be offering to you as simple ways to create whatever you need or desire.

Yes, indeed, *New Psychic Energy Power* is a magnificent ally to have on your team. And to make doubly sure you're controlling the flow of this incredible energy, I'll reveal to you the *New Psychic Energy Gestures* which direct this Cosmic flow.

In addition I'll gladly show you something I personally have found the most thrilling and satisfying of all: the *New Psychic Energy Healing Postures* which have turned sickness into blooming health.

There's still more, much more, including a guided tour of the *Astral City of New Psychic Energy Power* to whose builders this book is dedicated.

All I ask from you is a little patience. Follow me as I lead you, one pace at a time. You'll gain greater benefit more quickly as we take this whole thrilling journey together.

JAMES I. WAS "MIRACULOUSLY" HEALED

You will find this case history carefully worded. For excellent legal reasons I must make no claims which imply *New Psychic Energy Power* can cure diseases or other human malfunctions.

WHY THIS BOOK WILL FULFILL EVERY NEED

So I merely record the sequence of events which took place in the life of Seattle, Washington resident James I.

Seven years ago, bothered by recurring chest pains, fatigue, dizzy spells, shortness of breath and other distress, 65-year-old James I. underwent a full physical from his doctor.

Diagnosis was cardiovascular disease. Prognosis suggested it could be progressive. James was given a maximum of three years to live if he exercised moderation in practically everything.

Despite regular treatment and care, within two years James could not climb stairs; he could not indulge in even the slightest exertion without sitting down to rest for a long while afterward; his chest pains were more frequent, often running down his left arm; his ankles were painfully swollen; he was suffering double vision; and he had persistent headaches. In short, James seemed to be heading for invalidism and possible death.

Casting around for anything to alleviate his distress and possibly prolong his life, James encountered a proponent of cone and pyramid power. While continuing his orthodox medical treatment, James installed several cones and pyramids in his home as instructed.

Today James is fit and well. His heart condition has improved to the extent that he no longer suffers any of the symptoms which were threatening to lay him low. He jogs regularly, makes furniture in his home workshop, eats and sleeps well, travels regularly, and expects "to outlive that young doctor who said three years was the best I could hope for, back in 1971. Was I cured by medicine, or 'miraculously' healed? Frankly, I neither know nor care: I'm well again and that's all that matters."

The pyramid and cone techniques James employed are incorporated in this book.

YOU HAVE BEEN CHOSEN TO BENEFIT FROM
NEW PSYCHIC ENERGY POWER

I'm overjoyed that you have been chosen to prove the awesome abilities of *New Psychic Energy Power*. For you *have* been chosen, in a very real sense. I tell you solemnly that anyone who does not truly *need* the techniques and methods herein described will never even *see* this book.

This bedrock fact which I can hardly emphasize strongly enough is that Cosmic Forces have geared this assembly of paper, cloth, card and printing ink to arrive precisely when and where it will do the most good.

Have you fully understood that, Thou Chosen One? If so, read on, absorbing my words which have been composed for you personally. Apply the simple instructions and see your life change to true glory.

And herewith is a reassurance to those of you I know will write and ask, "Does *New Psychic Energy Power* conflict with my religion?"

I have more to say on that later, but be assured that *New Psychic Energy Power* is a name for one of the mystic and reverential powers of this Universe which God created. You will be attuning yourself with tides and streams of being as He intended you to. Your proof of that will be the holy peace which imbues your body and mind, and the beautiful happenings in your life which follow.

New Psychic Energy Power is a name coined for this day and age. I have no doubt that the Essenes, who may have taught Jesus his healing ministry, knew about *New Psychic Energy Power*. But they would have called it by some other name, since they spoke a language other than English.

What you call *New Psychic Energy Power* is unimportant. What *is* important is that you *use New Psychic Energy Power* to transform your whole being the way you wish it to be.

WHY THIS BOOK WILL FULFILL EVERY NEED

SKEPTICAL PENNY R. WAS CONVINCED
AFTER ONLY THREE DAYS

"Sure you can say it's a load of garbage if that's what you want to think. *New Psychic Energy Power* is not worried: it's as impersonal as the gasoline in your car. No amount of denying gasoline will work will prevent it from driving a properly tuned engine, and similarly denials of *New Psychic Energy Power's* abilities will have no effect.

"Everyone's entitled to his or her opinions. All I suggest is you're entitled to knock *New Psychic Energy Power* only after you've tried it."

The above is part of a discussion I had with Penny R., a very skeptical young journalist in Oregon. She *knew* that all psychic stuff is fakery at worst, self-delusion at best.

Who was I to argue with her? Shattering anyone's fondest beliefs is rank unkindness in my opinion. If she wanted to adhere to such ideas, I was not about to give her a hard time with disputation, refutation, case histories, and generally putting up a Federal case for the validity of *New Psychic Energy Power*.

But good for Penny! She grudgingly agreed it would not do her any harm to try a simple piece of *New Psychic Energy Power* work.

I asked her what she most wanted to achieve in her life. Something improbable, so that if it happened it would be a personal miracle.

"Tell *New Psychic Energy Power* to sell my novel," she said, smiling wryly. "I've offered it to 17 publishers, they've all rejected it and I'm thoroughly discouraged. My dream is to have a best-seller published. If that happens I'll send you a testimonial to the miraculous abilities of *New Psychic Energy Power.*

"Frankly, I expect this to fail and when nothing has happened within six months I'm going to write a blistering

WHY THIS BOOK WILL FULFILL EVERY NEED

'told-you-so' article about you and *New Psychic Energy Power* that will curl your hair."

She also insisted she was "not going to spend hours each day meditating, affirming, working spells or anything spooky like that." *New Psychic Energy Power* must do its work with a single two-minute "treatment" before she left my home.

A tall order. Nevertheless, confident *New Psychic Energy Power* would not let me down, I had her hold a best-seller by another author while she gazed at my *New Psychic Energy Generator*, the psychic tool described for you in Energy Circuit 2.

"Just pretend that's your name and title on the book you're holding," I said.

She laughed at the simplicity of it all, and left, still laughing.

My turn to laugh came when I received a telegram three days later: "I AM CONVINCED. NOVEL ACCEPTED AND PROPOSED AS BOOK OF THE MONTH FOR LARGE BOOK CLUB. MOVIE RIGHTS ALREADY BEING NEGOTIATED. NEW PSYCHIC ENERGY POWER IS A WINNER."

ATTAIN YOUR DREAMS WITH NEW PSYCHIC ENERGY POWER

Have you ever watched one of those TV movies where the hero or heroine has *everything*? Leisured and successful, he or she basks in adulation from others, enjoys a stimulating and unpressured life where a crook of the finger brings worshipping partners, fawning maitre d's and obsequious financial advisers on the run.

The penthouse, ranch, boats, helicopter, fine clothes, best wines, French cuisine and blooming health are the visible symbols of the fulfillment which can be attained.

Maybe you've dreamed about emulating one of those stars. Perhaps not down to the last detail—no one, for instance, is going to force an executive Lear jet on you if you

WHY THIS BOOK WILL FULFILL EVERY NEED

dislike flying—but in essence, you wish you had some of the attributes and success of the very rich.

New Psychic Energy Power will do that small thing for you, if that's your desire. We're going to learn how very soon. But above and beyond the status symbols, the jewels and the bulging bankroll, *New Psychic Energy Power* offers an even greater prize which is yours for the asking. That prize is peace and contentment, a reward which even some of the richest and most outwardly successful people spend their entire lives reaching for, yet fail to grasp.

All that's for you, if you'll come with me on a fascinating journey through the remainder of this book. In exchange for your companionship I'll show you the way to fulfillment. No messing, no half-baked theories, only proven techniques which I'll fully illustrate as we go along. Techniques which have taken ordinary people just like you and me sweeping to contentment. Instantly. Automatically.

This is a simple way to happiness, and you're already on your way there. I know: *New Psychic Energy Power* planned it that way!

Geof Gray-Cobb

Table of Contents

Why This Book Will Fulfill Every Need 7

Beyond Pyramid Power · "Everything came up roses" for previous loser Dexter D. · Gain your rightful rewards with New Psychic Energy Power · Betty S. soared from misery to total contentment · New Psychic Energy Power brings personal miracles · James K. was "miraculously" healed · You have been chosen to benefit from New Psychic Energy Power · Skeptical Penny R. was convinced after only three days · Attain your dreams with New Psychic Energy Power

Energy Circuit 1:
Attuning Your Life with Psychic Pyramidic Circuits 29

The North Face of Material Wealth · Karen C. moved from Skid Road to Beverly Hills · The East Face of Love and Peace of Mind · Potential suicide Clive O. found a new life · The South Face of Protection and Offense · Ecstatic Iris P. says, "I overcame insuperable odds" · The West Face of Health and Strength · Larry F. "threw away his crutches" · Drawing New Psychic Energy Power to you · All negatives faded into sublime happiness for Nancy E. · The first glorious signs of New Psychic Energy Power in action

Energy Circuit 2:
How to Make and Use Your New Psychic Pyramidic Generator 46

Assembling your New Psychic Energy Generator · Good news came for Theo S. within hours of making his New Psychic

24   *TABLE OF CONTENTS*

Energy Generator · Where to place your new Psychic Energy Generator · "My enemies packed up and left," states Gladys T. · What to expect from your New Psychic Energy Generator · Janke L. struck it rich · When your personal miracles will come true · Married to an alcoholic, yet Laura N. says "I'm in control". How does your New Psychic Energy Generator work? · Ludovic C. now knows "what happiness really is" · Earth, Air, Fire and Water symbols

Energy Circuit 3:
The North Face of Material Wealth 65

Defining your material needs · Edythe A. literally sailed to prosperity · Money and possessions are yours with the Golden Square of Prithevi · "The first time I've seen my bank manager smile," says Carl T · Create instant assets with the New Psychic Energy Image Technique · Lola V had a wad of hundred-dollar bills fall at her feet · Spark up your mundane life with the Northern Earth Application · Monotony "flew out of the window" for lucky Phil K. · Banish new debts forever with the Glacial Ring-Pass-Not · "In the black for the first time I can recall," writes Dorothy M. · Improve your gambling luck with the Amazing Triad Attunement

Energy Circuit 4:
The East Face of Love and Peace of Mind... 80

Decide on your love desires and they're yours · "I found my personal harem," says Ahmed N. · Automatic freedom from despair with the Blue Circle of Vayu · Carol Y. met Mr. Right after years of misery · Dispel loneliness with the Magnetic Pictorial Technique · Elwood R. now has "more friends than I know what to do with" · Bring a perfect lover with the Eastern Air Technique · "He's just what I've always dreamed about," says Emily G. · Find total contentment with Skyscraper Attraction · Terry V. was wrong when he thought he was too old for complete fulfillment · Enslave your love target with the Multiple Quadratic Encirclement

Energy Circuit 5:
The South Face of Protection and Offense.. 99

Attack and defense decisions are simple with New Psychic

TABLE OF CONTENTS

Energy Power · Pat Q. mysteriously vanquished her enemies · Nothing bad can touch you when you use the Scarlet Triangle of Tejas · "It's better than having a guardian angel," attests Reginald Y. · Overcoming opposition with the Sympathetic Portrayal Technique · Jean W. secured a coveted well-paid position · Dispel negative or evil conditions with the Southern Fire Technique · Floyd J. repelled a black magic attack · Defeating your enemies with the Sunshine Protection Routine · Judy I. says, "All my obstructions faded away like magic" · Bad is swiftly transformed into good when you employ the Mystic Pentafork Method

Energy Circuit 6:
The West Face of Health and Strength 119

Pyramid Energy Circuits and your doctor: an unbeatable team · Charlie G. is fit after being given six months to live · Health blossoms when you apply the Silver Crescent of Apas · "I've had no repeat of my arthritis pains," avows 83-year-old Eileen U. · Regain blooming youth with the Reverse Time Tableau · Walter B. was rejuvenated and mistaken for his own son · Expel pain and suffering with the Western Water Technique · Beverley L. can dance again now her varicose veins have disappeared · Your natural energies surge when you use the Mental Bridge Method · Earl M. remarried and fathered three sons at the age of 78 · Bodily and mental perfection can follow the application of the Six-Rayed Star Thought

Energy Circuit 7:
The New Psychic Pyramid Gestures 135

These secret gestures make New Psychic Energy Power flow · Annie D. made a lawyer change his mind in her favor · The simple Digital Triad Gesture · Joseph H. made the Digital Triad Gesture and survived a catastrophe · The Quartet of Protection and Miracles · Facing certain disaster, Tamara F. used the Quartet of Protection and Miracles and lived · What can New Psychic Energy Gestures do for you? · "I never thought they were that powerful," writes Waldo U. · When to use your New Psychic Energy Gestures · Mary J. has everything she wants, thanks to New Psychic Energy Gestures · All techniques are improved by adding New Psychic Energy Gestures

26 *TABLE OF CONTENTS*

Energy Circuit 8:
Your Three Facial Psychic Pyramidic Features 151

Nature has given you three prime New Psychic Energy Features · Rudolf E. "thought it was stupid" but changed his mind when miracles happened to him · Your Rhinal Energy Focus · "I'm miles ahead since using my Rhinal Energy Focus regularly," writes Jane O. · Your Optic-Glossal Energy Focus · Tom W. tripled his sales after learning about his Optic-Glossal Energy Focus · Locating your invisible Mandible-Pineal Energy Focus · Sue B. woke up profitable personal power by using her Mandible-Pineal Energy Focus · Making full use of your Facial New Psychic Energy Features · "The Facial New Psychic Energy Features knowledge has improved the quality of my life," says Saul P. · Your Facial New Psychic Energy Features will work for you 24 hours each and every day

Energy Circuit 9:
The New Psychic Pyramidic Healing Postures 173

How to combine these Postures with West Face Techniques · Previously spastic and apparently retarded Edie M. now leads a normal life · The Pedal-Patella Healing Triad · "I can now lift 200 pounds," attests accident victim Mel A. · The Finger Contact Tonus Technique · Chronic maladies left after Marilyn H. tried the Finger Contact Tonus Technique · The Cranial Cover New Psychic Energy Circuit · "They said I was dumb," writes Dick W., "but the Cranial Cover New Psychic Energy Circuit helped to alter that" · Detecting the flow of new Psychic Energy Power · Sandy A. zoomed from welfare to wealth · When to adopt your New Psychic Energy Healing Postures

Energy Circuit 10:
The Amazing New Psychic Pyramidic Cone . 188

The New Psychic Energy Cone focuses a specialized form of metaphysical power · "I was unsure what to do, says Lew B. "The New Psychic Energy Cone automatically brought me happiness" · Make a New Psychic Energy Cone—or just a "pretend" one: equally effective in startling results · Ruth W. imagined New Psychic Energy Cones and good fortune ar-

TABLE OF CONTENTS

27

rived · How to visualize a 24-hour New Psychic Energy Cone anywhere · "I'm convinced my New Psychic Energy Cones helped clean up my debts," writes Hank G. · Your New Psychic Energy Cone has unlimited power for you to use · "Miracles are mine," states Gloria M., New Psychic Energy Cone user · How, when and where to use your New Psychic Energy Cone

Energy Circuit 11:
Creating Your Total New Psychic Pyramidic Environment.................................. 200

Making your Akashic List of Desires and Needs · "My Akashic List came true like one-two-three," writes Ronald D. · Which techniques to use for most brilliant results · Marion S. "got it right first time" and is now a happy millionaire · A quick trip together around the Four Faces · The Horus Future Technique showed her what numbers to play · How to work the Horus Future Technique · Tom A. was "nowhere" a year ago; now he's "on top of the heap" · Points to watch to refine your New Psychic Energy Power

Energy Circuit 12:
Journey to the Apex for a Lifetime of Miracles 215

The journey together so far · The Astral City of New Psychic Energy Power · "Visiting" the Astral City turned life around for Scott B. · Explore the Astral City without lifting a finger · Peggy R. learned secret news in the Astral City · Creating life miracles by visiting the Astral City · Also-ran Mike H. is a big winner today · New Psychic Energy Power combines perfectly with your religion and philosophies · Terri L. tells her success story in her own words · Reach out for it and New Psychic Energy Power will bring it to you

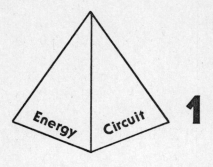

Attuning Your Life with Psychic Pyramidic Circuits

Our material world is built on the power and stability of the number four. The ancients saw everything composed of the four "elements"—Earth, Air, Fire and Water, and the four "qualities"—hot, cold, wet and dry.

We fix our positions in the world with four directions—north, south, east and west. Our measurements of material things depend on the four attributes of length, width, thickness and duration. We spend much of our life between four walls. The sacred cross, with all its spiritual and mystic powers, has four arms.

I could continue adding to the list which shows how the number four is important to us—but what I would especially like you to notice is the way in which four is built into the pyramids, those monuments to Egyptian pharaohs who enjoyed wealth and power which has never been equaled in modern times. Compared with the gold and treasures of even the lowliest pharaoh, Howard Hughes was a welfare case!

A pyramid stands firmly on its base of four sides, usually arranged to face precisely north, south, east and west. Both

30   *ATTUNING YOUR LIFE*

occult and scientific researchers have shown us that the act of creating a pyramid does something wonderful to the local space-time continuum. For natural reasons which we have yet to fully unravel, building a pyramid focuses unseen energies.

Even more excitingly, those energies can be used by anyone who has the necessary know-how. And by the time you've finished reading this book, you will have that know-how, and the results are in your hands to create whatever kind of world you wish to live in.

We could theorize that the construction of pyramids was what made the pharaohs so tremendously wealthy. So, by extension, you and I are going to build pyramids for you, harness and channel the energies, and you can become as rich as any pharaoh.

And I speak not merely about cash and possessions. You can become rich in health, rich in happiness, rich in power, rich in all the intangibles without which money is just so much printed paper.

You're truly being given the chance to become a millionaire, with a bottomless purse containing all that so many seek, and so few find. Our path together can bring you priceless peace of mind, with all the material advantages necessary to enjoy it, in a vital and healthy body which you may have thought was eclipsed when your youth faded.

Our first step toward that sparkling dream is to look at the four pyramid faces, identifying the special powers of each face. And I would like you to realize a very important psychic truth at this point.

Pyramid Energy works on your mind and body, invisibly, and the very act of reading these words and thinking about them will place vital key phrases in your head, ready to use Pyramid Energy to bring your miracles to pass.

You may have been anticipating that I would tell you to build a pyramid in your living room, or in your back yard, and live inside the structure. You can do that if you wish—we will, in fact, be considering how to build a small pyramid in the next section of this book. But I tell you solemnly and truly that

ATTUNING YOUR LIFE

although having a pyramid you can see, touch and experience is very useful, by far the most important alignment with Pyramid Energy occurs *in your mind*, easily and automatically as you read my words.

As we proceed, study the case histories with care. I have selected them carefully, describing at some length how various people found happiness. Many of them followed precisely the techniques we are learning, so you can discover a great deal of how to apply these methods by observing the subjects in the case histories.

My idea is that you should, where applicable, emulate their methods of work with *New Psychic Energy Power*— examples being worth many pages of detailed explanation.

THE NORTH FACE OF MATERIAL WEALTH

North in the occult tradition is identified with the ancient element of Earth and the mighty Angel Uriel.

The Earth element is material and solid, and by tuning in to the *North Face Psychic Energy Tide*, you align yourself with acquiring whatever material things you need, such as money, real estate, furnishings, clothes ... any and all of life's necessities and luxuries you can see and touch.

It's all amazingly simple. In the following sections I'll guide you accurately into the main stream of the North Face Tide and let its bountiful energy sweep your inner dreams into tangible, material form.

KAREN C. MOVED FROM SKID ROAD TO BEVERLY HILLS

Although you'll often find me saying that health, strength and peace of mind should take priority over the acquisition of hard cash, some case histories are marked exceptions to that rule.

32 *ATTUNING YOUR LIFE*

The case of Karen C. exemplifies the point. We can see how she chose to establish priorities about what she most needed. In her case, it worked admirably.

Karen came from a part of Harlem which even by local standards was reckoned to be rundown. Enough has been written, filmed, exposed and exploited for us to realize the squalor of her life without going into detail.

"Don't forget the stink," Karen said. "You can show bad things on TV to other folks, but you gotta live there to know how it smells. You gotta be part of it to feel the violence and hopelessness. You gotta be Harlem-born before you truly know about those diff'rent strokes."

Karen, now a suave and polished lady of leisure, is working with a well-known Los Angeles writer on her life story, so I must not infringe their copyright by writing at length about her. Heroin, street-walking, pimps, dirt, hunger and pain all form part of a past she's put behind her now. A desperate, lost existence where she never knew, and often did not care, if she would see the next gray light of dawn.

"I knew there was only one way out for me," she said, "and that was through the doors of the morgue. I figured the kind of miracle I needed to escape that hopelessness was reserved for good people."

Destiny had other ideas. One night Karen got talking to a trio of musicians in a bar.

"They were far out," she said. "They'd just been offered a fine gig uptown, and they said their pyramid had done it for them. See, they had this little cardboard gizmo on the table with bits of colored paper stuck to it.

"I was stoned out of my gourd at the time, and when they told me to look at the yellow square on one side and make a wish I just yelled, 'Karen needs a million bucks to get her out of this s**t.' Like they were cool guys and I played along with their funning."

Karen proved to be a classic example which sometimes occurs of an almost instant miracle happening.

One of her clients next day had just come back from Canada.

ATTUNING YOUR LIFE

"When I counted the money he laid on me I found he'd also given me a lottery ticket tucked in with the greenbacks," she said. "I kept it tucked in my bra until the draw was held."

You're ahead of me! Yes, Karen was a big winner. Her ticket matched one of the $1,000,000 prizes. Even with the deflated Canadian dollar, Karen suddenly owned around $850,000.

"That was close enough to a million for me," she said. "Thank the good Lord I'd learned to handle money and knew my way around. I invested enough to bring me a healthy yearly income. Then I'm not saying any more than that I bought myself a piece of respectability in Beverly Hills. Nobody knows much about where I've come from or how I'm fixed. They'll find out when my book hits the market, but that's going to happen when I'm ready, not before."

Of necessity, this case history is succinct, but you have the salient features. One touch of the musician's pyramid (which was identical to the *New Psychic Energy Generator* you're going to build for yourself) and Karen's troubles were over.

THE EAST FACE OF LOVE AND PEACE OF MIND

Personally, I consider this face, aligned with the East Face Tide, to be more important than the North Face. Material possessions are fine if you're able to enjoy them, but I'd like you to consider an occult maxim which states: "If you do not have love and peace of mind, you cannot gain benefits from the material things of life—and no matter what possessions you acquire, they cannot *make* you peaceful and loved."

Stated another way, we say, "Money will not buy happiness." That's true. I often receive letters from my readers who tell me, "If I had $10,000 I'd be able to find peace of mind." Sorry, but that's not necessarily so: money can help a lot, but it's by no means a surefire path to satisfaction and fulfillment.

What *is* more certain to lead to such a desirable state is aligning yourself with the *East Face Psychic Energy Tide*,

34   *ATTUNING YOUR LIFE*

drawing on the traditional power of the Air element, watched over (so it is said) by the power of Angel Raphael.

Whether you're rich or poor, I urge you to tune to the East Face Tide to bring you love and peace of mind as a prime move, even before you use the North Face Tide to bring you a sack of gold pieces!

POTENTIAL SUICIDE CLIVE O. FOUND A NEW LIFE

I am indebted to Clive O. for allowing me access to his personal diary to illustrate how the *East Face of Love and Peace of Mind* was instrumental in bringing him back from the brink of madness and suicide.

These relevant extracts, transcribed verbatim, reveal his case more graphically than any narrative I could write.

NOV. 17: The pain is worse today. Dr. B. says it is imagination and wants me to see Dr. Z. I won't go: Dr. Z is evil and would kill me. Yet I know I have a creeping cancerous condition eating its way into my brain. Martha says she will leave if I don't stop screaming in my sleep. Dreams very bad last night. I'm tired; nerves are shot. Getting drunk doesn't help.

NOV. 20: Martha packed and left today. She says not to call her until I'm prepared to accept help. How can I get help from that Thing hiding in dark corners? I see it out of the corner of my eye but when I look directly at it flicks away to the side. Paid September rent: must call the bank and tell them not to bounce the check.

NOV. 22: I saw it! The Thing is revolting. A slimy yellow and green shape with a black, gaping maw opening on limbo. It intends to swallow me while I sleep. So I stay awake and it lurks on the floor at my feet as I write this. If I don't look at it straight it stays still and I can feel it pulsing slowly with the alien life of the Pit. I threw a cup at it but it was too quick. The cup smashed and I cut my hand on the pieces. The Thing lapped up my spilled blood.

NOV. 27: The money's all gone. The telephone has

ATTUNING YOUR LIFE

been disconnected. Electricity and gas will be cut off in three days if I don't pay. Tried for a job downtown but I shake so hard I can't even shave properly. Why will no one help me? What do I do? The Thing still waits. It followed me to the bus today, and was still there when I came back.

DEC 1: It's closer. I hear the Thing now, making obscene sucking and slobbering sounds. I almost wish it would hurry and finish its awful game. I'm also hungry. Sitting in the dark and cold will be hell when the sun has gone. The shadows close in. Will I see another dawn?

DEC. 2: Very weak and feverish. I fought the Thing last night. Fell on it and stabbed it a hundred times with a steak knife. It hissed and wriggled away, leaving a trail like a giant slug. It will come closer again. It sits on the far side of the scars in the floor where I stabbed. Someone was screaming today. I stopped when I realized it was me.

DEC. 3: A man came to the door. Said he was from welfare. I wouldn't let him in. He shouted through the door about talking to me, help and hospital. Too late for that. I pulled the table across the door and he went away. I'm going to escape the Thing tonight. I can already feel the icy bite of the razor as it slices my throat to bring the pulse of warm blood throbbing my life away. I expect the Thing will enjoy its meal. But what if it follows me across the void into death itself? God, would evil incarnate pursue me for eternity?

DEC. 4: Martha called last night just as I was getting ready to end it all. I wouldn't go with her. Didn't talk much because the Thing was listening. It stayed behind Martha all the time she was here so she didn't see it. She said she would send two men around who would take me to a better place. I laughed and said they'd better bring lunch for the Thing because it would be coming along with me wherever I went. I made her leave. Strange, I haven't seen the Thing yet today and it's almost noon. I feel a mite calmer. Wonder why I decided to wait another day before using the razor? Almost forgot. Martha left a kerosene heater and candles. She also put a little pyramid thing on the table. She said it was a protective charm against the Thing. I need more than a charm to keep the Thing away.

> *DEC. 5: The Thing has been absent for 36 hours. Could it all have been in my mind? I've decided suicide would be stupid, solving nothing.*
>
> *DEC. 6: Cold, bright day. I went out for the first time this week. Christmas is coming, yet so many people look sad and worried. Wonder why? Life is good. Still no job but I know I'll find one.*
>
> *DEC. 7: Money in my pocket! Worked six hours at the market. If I make out good there's permanent work with prospects for me. Reading what I wrote in November, I wonder where my head was at. I must have been a little crazy. All behind me now. Martha says we'll keep the pyramid charm on the stereo. She's coming back to me tomorrow.*

Clive continues to thrive. He's now a well-adjusted man, happily settled in a good job. He has had no recurrence of his hallucinations and fears.

THE SOUTH FACE OF PROTECTION AND OFFENSE

The powerful Angel Michael is said to reign over the South Face of the pyramid and the element Fire is associated with this face.

By attuning yourself with the *South Face Psychic Energy Tide* you align yourself symbolically with all the forceful things fire can do.

Like electricity, fire is a magnificent servant but a dangerous master. Fire can destroy, causing pain and loss, or it can be used to drive engines, or to turn raw meat or dough into delicious foodstuffs.

By tuning in to the South Face Tide, you become the symbolic master or mistress of Fire, being able to use its energy to perform personal miracles.

I hasten to add two points. First, we are talking about the *idea* of Fire and its powers; no way am I recommending actual use of arson or firearms as solutions to any problems.

ATTUNING YOUR LIFE

Second, before using the awesome powers of the South Face Tide, consider all other solutions.

You understand that the South Face Tide gives you the ultimate power to destroy anyone or anything. This can literally be a dangerous power trip for some people, and bring hazardous consequences which take much work to turn around to positivity again.

Instead of angrily deciding to burn your enemy to a crisp with symbolic Fire, a better course by far is to use the Fire energy to erect a barrier to *protect* yourself.

Iris P. in the next case history from my files illustrates precisely how the South Face Tide can best be used.

ECSTATIC IRIS P. SAYS, "I OVERCAME INSUPERABLE ODDS!"

Appropriately matching her name, Iris P. owns a small flower shop in California. She runs it single-handed.

"I'd scrimped and saved for years to buy my business," she said. "With the aid of a bank loan and with perhaps more enthusiasm than experience I opened the doors and became my own person for the very first time in my life."

Despite long hours of dedicated toil, Iris found making a profit hard. Income always seemed to be slightly less than outgo. Unpaid bills began slipping beyond their credit time limits and interest charges grew. She had to arrange to miss a payment on her bank loan.

"It was all going sour on me," she said. "The big stores who ran flower and garden departments were also feeling the pinch of depressed business, but they could afford to absorb losses for a while. I had no other income to fall back on."

Soon Iris was hovering on the brink of bankruptcy. Creditors were pressing hard, she was behind with her rent, and the local newspapers would allow her no more credit for advertisements.

"I became nervous and fatigued. I was heading for failure and sickness, but what could I do?"

38   *ATTUNING YOUR LIFE*

Resting sadly in bed one Sunday, trying to recover from the exhaustion of the week and store up energy for the new battle to survive which would begin next day, Iris idly flicked the pages of a book a friend had loaned her.

"I had had little time for reading, but by then I'd sold my TV and stereo to meet more pressing matters, so I became absorbed in the book," she said. "It was about the secret power of pyramids. I guess it was as much hopelessness as interest that had me make a little pyramid and try the method described."

What Iris had found was a South Face Tide technique which others had used to protect themselves from adversity.

"Staring at a colored piece of folded cardboard seemed futile," she said. "Yet it had a strange calming effect on me. For the first time in weeks I did not cry myself to sleep. I remember telling myself that worrying myself into an early grave would not help a bit."

Iris took her pyramid to her store next day, and was surprised to find three customers waiting to buy flowers.

"They told me one of the big stores down the road had closed its floral department because the manager had decided they'd put enough money into a losing sector," Iris said. "That was good news. I'd no sooner served my waiting customers than I had a phone call asking me to arrange all the flowers for a big wedding.

"Business turned positive from that day on. I acquired a reputation for reliability, willingness and fair prices, and was able to pay off the bank loan five months later.

"I keep the little pyramid on a shelf behind the counter. As business continues to expand I certainly feel it gives me solid protection from bad luck and has helped me overcome insuperable odds."

THE WEST FACE OF HEALTH AND STRENGTH

Watched over by the power of benevolent Angel Gabriel,

ATTUNING YOUR LIFE

the *West Face Psychic Energy Tide* is identified with the element of Water.

No matter how many pills, potions and nostrums you may have in your home, none of them is worth a wooden nickel unless you use them in tune with the West Face Tide which governs health and strength.

Strange as it may seem to some, your body was designed by its Creator to be strong and healthy. Given half a chance, a diseased or sick body will automatically battle hard to return to health. Any honest doctor will tell you that in many cases his prescriptions are merely assists to make the patient comfortable *while the body heals itself.*

The doctor does not *cure* you of a malady: *you* do that by giving your body a chance to use its miraculous self-healing powers. More and more, medical science is discovering that many diseases are caused by our mistreatment and outright poisoning of our physical bodies. And that poisoning is not only physical: even *mental* "poisoning" can occur, by entertaining powerful negative thoughts which eventually appear as *physical* disease.

Some researchers now believe that even the dreaded scourge of cancer can be defeated by using mind power to supplement medical treatment and give the body maximum chances to expel the cancerous body cells and replace them with healthy ones.

All the above can be summed up in this psychic method by suggesting you attune yourself with the West Face Tide. Allowing that energy to flow through you brings natural healing energies to a peak, so that aches, pains and weaknesses quickly become things of the past for you.

LARRY F. "THREW AWAY HIS CRUTCHES"

Badly injured in a car accident, 26-year-old Larry F. spent three full years going from one doctor and specialist to the next. Six operations later his surgeon told Larry everything possible had been done to repair his injured spine.

"They'd taken out a piece of my hip bone and used it to weld several crushed vertebrae," he said. "A silver pin held my hip in place, while my left knee was a jigsaw of slowly mending bone splinters.

"The pain was less than it had been before the first operation but I had to walk with crutches. I was not about to play football again: limping to the john was about my limit of strenuous activity!"

Larry resigned himself to spending the rest of his life on crutches, with the specter of a wheelchair existence hovering if his fractured body should take a turn for the worse.

"The doctors said is was only a matter of time before the repairs wore out," he said. "They said I should be prepared for even more restricted movement before I reached my 40's."

With his previously athletic life totally disbarred, Larry had to find other leisure pastimes.

"My pal Bob was into pyramid experiments," Larry said. "We'd meet a couple of times a week and discuss the latest research into such powers. I was very doubtful about it all, despite the written reports and evidence. I could not see how building a particular shape which had no working parts could have any effect on its surroundings."

Nevertheless, Larry agreed to be the "guinea pig" for Bob in a West Face Tide experiment.

"We used a six-inch pyramid, put the symbols and signs on it and I spent five minutes every day studying the West Face and remembering my earlier days when I was top scorer with the local football team," Larry said. "Two weeks later I took my first unsupported step since the accident. I naturally continued with my previous therapies, but I find it a strange coincidence that the first real signs I might be on the mend came after I began the pyramid work."

Progress was rapid. Larry's knee regained full mobility.

"My spine seemed less rigid, I was waking in the morning free of pain and I could walk several steps without aid," he said. "I was still very creaky, though, and I was glad to sit down after my brief excursions. But compared to my previous incapacity, I felt like a new man.

ATTUNING YOUR LIFE **41**

"I gained enough confidence and endurance to throw away my crutches. I'm gradually beginning to resume my old life. You're unlikely to see me scoring a field goal this year, but I honestly feel that's a later possibility."

DRAWING NEW PSYCHIC ENERGY POWER TO YOU

Aligning yourself with *New Psychic Energy Power* is simplicity itself. In detail, I'll be explaining how to do it later in this book.

In essence, you're tuning your mind and body to unseen vibrations—and it's no more tedious or difficult than tuning your radio or TV to your local studios by pushing a switch and turning a knob. This *New Psychic Energy Power* method shows you, exactly and precisely, which mental and physical "knobs" to turn, and thus effortlessly change your life.

You may be wondering why we're going through this preamble before actually finding out *what* to do to become wealthy, peaceful, protected and healthy. You may even be tempted to skim through this section, seeking the practical techniques further on. Please refrain from skipping chunks of this book: if any parts had been unnecessary, I would have been pleased to leave them out, if only to reduce the sheer toil of all this typing and thus get the book to you more quickly.

This introductory stuff is very necessary, and I've already indicated why. I'm planting ideas in your mind, preparing you for the miracles to come.

Believe it: the "tuning in" has already begun, even though you've turned only a few pages of this book so far.

ALL NEGATIVES FADED INTO SUBLIME HAPPINESS FOR NANCY E.

Nancy E. was one of the unfortunate people who lost their homes and possessions in the 1978 floods which devastated parts of North America.

ATTUNING YOUR LIFE

"I went down with bronchitis while we were in temporary housing provided by the authorities," she said. "We had carried no insurance, my husband and I were on welfare, and we'd never had children who might have helped us through the crisis.

"Not too long after the flood was a memory, we were deep in trouble. We'd rented a furnished room, I was still wheezing and under par. My husband had been able to find a job with a removal firm even though at 64 he was not really fit to carry heavy loads.

"Then the tax people were bugging us for $748 they said we owed from last year. I heard my aunt was desperately sick, yet we could not afford to visit with her. A final blow came when my husband tore a knee ligament and was laid up in bed. More bills piled up, we were evicted from our room and we just did not know which way to turn."

The future was dark for Nancy and her husband. Both sick, no money, little food, growing debts and no respite in sight.

"Desperation is just a word until you truly live with it," Nancy said. "We could not adjust to being residents of an old people's home for the indigent where we found shelter. I used to pray to God each night, asking for a miracle."

Pyramids came into Nancy's life unexpectedly.

"One person in the hostel whom I found totally peaceful and satisfied was old George," Nancy said. "He was 92 and still quietly enjoying life. He used to say he'd done everything and now he was ready to meet his Maker whenever He chose to call. Until then he'd wait patiently, playing with his 'toys.'

"He showed his toys to me: little card pyramids with signs and colored symbols on them. He'd spend hours just gazing at them. He said he could travel all over the universe in his mind while he sat looking at a pyramid."

Nancy thought this was all the harmless delusion of a senile mind, but one afternoon she joined George in his favorite corner, and listened while he told her how to tune in to the power of the pyramids.

ATTUNING YOUR LIFE **43**

"As I looked at each symbol I found different emotions stirring. I felt more peaceful, healthier, protected and hopeful. George grinned when I said it was all suggestion. His answer was that did it matter what it was if it helped to make life happier?"

That single session with George started a train of marvelous events for Nancy.

"Two days later George died quietly in his sleep, smiling happily at some private joke," Nancy said. "He'd recently written his will, and we were surprised to find he'd left everything he owned to us. He'd written that I was the only person who had not poked fun at his pyramids, so he left them to me.

"We were touched at his gesture, but amazed at what followed. He also willed us the contents of a bank deposit box to help us a little."

The deposit box proved to be a treasure trove. It contained a cache of antique jewelry, several hundred thousand dollars in old currency dating back decades, and the deeds to a luxurious apartment block which was being fully managed and maintained by a paid staff with the profits mailed to George each month.

"In the box was a note," Nancy related. "It said: 'Enjoy all this, whoever claims it. I had no need for it, for my pyramids opened the doors to greater riches than man can provide.'

"Moving suddenly from abject poverty to opulence was almost too much to comprehend. But we managed it. And we keep George's pyramids in pride of place in our penthouse."

THE FIRST GLORIOUS SIGNS OF NEW PSYCHIC ENERGY POWER IN ACTION

You want proof, eh? You seek physical evidence, perhaps, that all this talk of Psychic Power Tides and Energies is not just a figment of my fevered imagination.

44   *ATTUNING YOUR LIFE*

I agree that taking my words on trust entails a suspension of disbelief, and some of you will feel you cannot wait to actually prove out these Psychic Energy Tides by waiting for the miraculous results.

So here is a small test, a simple technique, which enables you to *feel New Psychic Energy Power* within you, so you know it's just waiting to change your most hopeless dreams into stupendous reality.

What part of your body is unhealthy? A pain, a twinge, any malfunction will do. Headache, kidney stone, toothache, cut, bruise, blister, carbuncle, pimple, charley horse or creaking joint—some part of you is not working quite as it should. Even if you're the world's greatest health buff, you're certain to have a tooth cavity, receding hair, a hang nail ... something you'd like to see cured.

All right: bare the skin over the hurt and lay your hand on it. Which hand? The most convenient one; it's not important which. Both hands if you like—this works well for indigestion, for instance, with both hands laid across the pain, with fingers touching.

Now breathe deeply.[1] Really deeply, about ten times, inflating your lungs to their fullest, then exhaling until you can almost feel your stomach wall touch your spine. Make the breaths faster than usual—force the air in and out a bit. You should be able to complete the ten breaths in less than one minute.

While you're doing this, and afterward as you allow your breathing to return to its normal rate and depth, feel what's happening under and in your hand.

You'll detect a prickling sensation, a tingling in your palm or fingers. Or maybe you'll feel a coolness or extra heat under the hand. Certainly you'll feel something.

Physically, the deep breathing has cleaned carbon dioxide gas from your bloodstream, temporarily changing the

---

[1] If you have a heart condition and have been told or suspect that deep breathing is dangerous to your well-being, disregard this test.

ATTUNING YOUR LIFE

electrical balance of your body fluids, and thus altering the sensitivity of your nerves.

You're feeling a symptom of *New Psychic Energy Power* doing its amazing work. If you had a pain when you started, you may have felt it increase slightly before it began to fade. Skin blemishes will heal quicker than usual with a similar daily application of *New Psychic Energy Power*. No matter what's wrong with you, regular treatment as described will begin to tune your body to heal itself.[2]

That was simple enough, agreed? And nothing to come is any more complicated or difficult, and you've now mastered a vital part of the West Face Tide techniques. We'll be looking at them in greater depth in Energy Circuit 6, later in this book.

But before that, let us move to Energy Circuit 2, which tells you about the miraculous *New Psychic Energy Generator.*

---

[2]This technique must *not* be used to replace professional health care and treatment. Use it in addition to your doctor's treatment if you need to be under medical care.

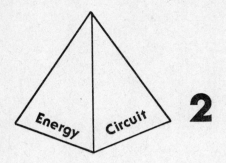

How to Make and Use Your New Psychic Pyramidic Generator

This section brings us to the construction of a simple little artifact with awesome powers. It's going to involve you in a minor amount of work with pencil, cardboard, scissors and tape or glue, but I assure you the small time and effort you invest in this can bring dividends out of all proportion to the physical energy and thought you expend in constructing it.

ASSEMBLING YOUR NEW PSYCHIC ENERGY GENERATOR

On the facing page you'll see Figure 1, made up of four triangles. This is the pattern for your *New Psychic Energy Generator*, and the very first *vital* point I wish to make is this: DO NOT CUT THE DIAGRAM FROM THE PAGE to make your Generator.

The reason is that on the other side of that page the text of this book continues. If you cut the page, two things will occur: first, you'll lose some of these instructions which you may need to refer to later. Second, and more important, if you

MAKE YOUR PSYCHIC PYRAMIDIC GENERATOR

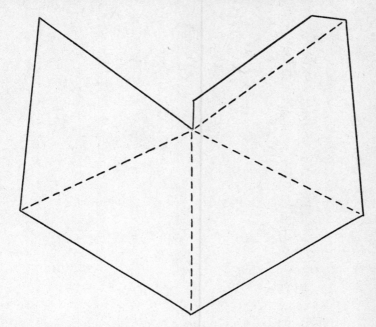

FIGURE 1: Pattern for New Psychic Energy Generator

construct your New Psychic Energy Generator from the diagram itself, when your Generator is completed it will have printing all over the inside of it. This is not the idea: the inside of your Generator needs to be blank.

In summary, *making your Generator by cutting the pattern from this book will be useless: the Generator will fail to operate as it should.*

Your first task, then, is to trace the diagram on to a sheet of thin card, which need be no larger than four inches square. What thickness should the card be? Stiff but not rigid is the answer; about the thickness of the cover of the average paperback book, or a trifle thicker, is about right.

If you do not happen to have such a piece of plain card lying around your home, ask your local shoe store for a shoe box they're going to throw out—the card used to make that is ideal for your purpose.

48   *MAKE YOUR PSYCHIC PYRAMIDIC GENERATOR*

The color of the card is unimportant, although white, gray or neutral buff is probably best.

When you've drawn your diagram on the card, cut around the outline and you're almost through. Lay the card flat on the table and score the four dotted lines with the point of the scissors, denting the card to make it easy to fold along the dotted lines.

Last, fold the card away from you at the four dotted lines, and tuck the end tab under the triangle on the left, securing it with a dab of glue or a bit of tape.

There, looking like my sketch in Figure 2, opposite, is your basic *New Psychic Energy Generator* in the shape of a small pyramid.

It's intended to stand on any flat surface, on its open base, just like its gigantic brother, the Great Pyramid of Gizeh—and you're going to find, despite its diminutive size that your Generator has enormous powers for good.

GOOD NEWS CAME FOR THEO S. WITHIN HOURS OF MAKING HIS NEW PSYCHIC ENERGY GENERATOR

Theo S. is pleased to be included in this book as a prime example of what can happen as soon as you begin to tune in to Pyramid Power and its higher energies. However, Theo would prefer his true identity to remain secret. To observe that request I have changed some salient features in this case history to make quite sure he is unrecognizable.

Theo (now known by a stage name you'd instantly recognize) was not always the popular star and show host he is today. He can easily recall his many years of struggling to stay alive. If you'd told him only three short years ago that today he'd be hosting his own nationwide TV program, applauded by audiences and loved by viewers, he'd have smiled sweetly and told you to go peddle your fantasy pills some place else.

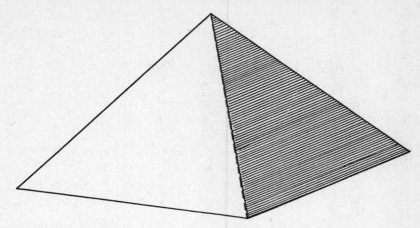

FIGURE 2: Basic New Psychic Energy Generator

Because of rheumatoid fever, Theo was a retiring, timid child. Through his teen years he never showed initiative or spark.

"I was the butt of bullies," he says. "If they were feeling like taking out their frustrations on anyone, nine times in ten it was Theo who got roughed up.

"My parents divorced when I was 12 and I spent years in several foster homes. I did two years in jail for an alleged embezzlement which was a frame-up."

After coming out of his cell, Theo had much trouble finding work. He knows firsthand that despite rehabilitation promises, an ex-con carries a stigma for the rest of his life.

"I wanted to enter real estate but my license was refused when they found out I had a record," he said. "Time after time employers turned me down. I was tempted to live up to their expectations that an ex-con can never go straight. I'd have really taken up crime as a living, but I was afraid to."

So Theo persisted in seeking straight employment. Eventually he found work in a small radio station in New Jersey.

"I swept the floor, carried garbage, made coffee for the d-j's, greased the station truck, filed scripts and oiled

50   MAKE YOUR PSYCHIC PYRAMIDIC GENERATOR

typewriters," he said. "About the only menial job around the station I was not called on to do was to wipe the manager's nose."

Toiling 48 hours a week, Theo pulled down just enough to keep body and soul together.

"Lucky I was not aspiring to any luxuries," he said. "I was too busy working to need a car for joy-riding, and glad to sleep rather than go out on the town."

Theo's life continued unchanged for months, with no prospects of any kind of break.

The factor that coincided with Theo's life alteration was the visit of a psychic on one of the station's hot-line shows.

"During her discussion on air she was asked by a caller what she thought about the power of pyramids," Theo related. "Specifically, the caller described a combination of pyramid, symbols and sigils he'd put together which he said brought him good luck.

"The psychic was enthusiastic, so figuring I needed some good luck I built a pyramid and showed it to her before she left the station."

The busy psychic hurried out to her waiting cab.

"That's good," she called. "Now watch what happens!"

The first thing Theo noticed happening was a snow-storm, three feet deep and drifting. The cabs and buses headed for the garage and Theo was marooned at the station. The snow also prevented the evening shift of radio people getting to work.

"It was sheer necessity and shortage of warm bodies which prompted the station manager to tell me to get my head down and sleep and then take over a record show at midnight," Theo said. "He told me all I had to do was put discs on the turntable and switch in commercial cassettes and pre-packaged news tapes at intervals called out in a script."

By dawn Theo was totally bored with the routine and decided to take over a live microphone and talk to the waking city.

MAKE YOUR PSYCHIC PYRAMIDIC GENERATOR   51

"I just went ad lib, played a little music from records I liked, told a joke or two, gave a spoof weather forecast, held an imaginary interview with Santa Claus, handling his voice as well as my own—silly things like that," Theo said. "I was having fun, and I figured no one was listening anyway."

Theo was still going strong when the day shift of announcers and staff showed. When the receptionist arrived she found her switchboard lit up like a Christmas tree with incoming calls. Those calls, all wanting to know who the great guy on the air was, continued long after Theo had handed over to a regular staffer.

Theo had caught the public's imagination. By some magic of warmth, personality and timing he was a hit. His own talk show started the following week, and his city had a day of mock mourning when he left for bigger and better things on the West Coast.

"I took my pyramid, of course," he said. "And I've never stopped going up since. Money? More than I need. Fame? Awards fill my den. Lovelife? Perfect. Contentment? Supreme!"

The pyramid Theo built is identical to the *New Psychic Energy Generator* I've shown you how to build. Truly identical: Theo was kind enough to show his pyramid to me and allow me to sketch it.

WHERE TO PLACE YOUR NEW PSYCHIC ENERGY GENERATOR

Despite its possibly humble beginnings as a discarded shoe box, you now own a true psychic tool to assist you in your search for happiness. Part of its potency, by the way, is due to the fact that you built it for yourself; all experienced psychic workers acknowledge the greater efficiency of artifacts which are self-made.

So although it's possible for you to buy a small pyramid, or even to have someone do this simple card-folding job for

MAKE YOUR PSYCHIC PYRAMIDIC GENERATOR

you, you're far better served by custom-building your Generator your own way, putting your time, labor and thoughts into it.

Your Generator forms a focus for the energies you will be using to reshape your life, so you need to find a place for it to sit and absorb and radiate. Some of the psychic techniques require you to sit and look at it, so you need to give it a few inches of space on a shelf, windowsill or table where it can sit relatively undisturbed.

Yes, you can put it away in a closet or drawer between times, but I've found it best to allocate a spot for your Generator and leave it there.

The final spot you choose for your Generator's "home" should be in a quiet room (if you have one!), away from the distractions of the TV, stereo or radio. Your kitchen, dining area or bedroom are fine.

Place your Generator as far as feasible from electrical sockets and trailing extension cords to appliances or swag lamps. If you happen to have aluminum siding on your residence, do not place your Generator against the outside wall of the room; aluminum has been found to screen off some of your Generator's more powerful energies.

Lastly, arrange your Generator to face the four points of the compass. That is, if it was out in the open, the rising sun would shine on its east face. Arranged that way, two of the parallel sides will run north and south. You can set it with a hiker's compass if you wish, or find the North Star on a clear night and use that as a reference point.

This orientation matches your Generator to the Earth's magnetic field which runs north and south.

"MY ENEMIES PACKED UP AND LEFT," STATES GLADYS T.

Gladys T. is much like the rest of us. She works hard, tries not to hurt her fellow beings, cares for her husband in sickness and in health as she promised at their wedding 20

MAKE YOUR PSYCHIC PYRAMIDIC GENERATOR 53

years ago. She is doing her best to raise her children to be respectable citizens, she watches her budget carefully, and she recognizes the give and take necessary to a peaceful community.

"So I was totally shocked when a group of local residents ganged up against me," she said. "To this day I'm unaware what I did or said to earn their enmity unless they were jealous of our steady progress.

"All I know is a steady hate campaign began against us. My children were harassed on the school bus. Someone threw a dead cat on our lawn the week after our garbage pails, awaiting pickup, had been spilled across the driveway.

"Then a brick crashed through the living room window while we were shopping. Those were the material things that went on, but the rumors that began about us were worse.

"People were whispering I was bouncing checks, something I have never done. Yet that rumor alone was enough to close off credit in the town for me."

Harassing phone calls began at all hours of the day and night. When Gladys' husband answered, an obviously disguised voice told him obscene lies about what his wife was doing while he was at work.

"Our ornamental hedge died when acid was poured on the roots," Gladys related. "More foul rumors circulated, and even my friends were crossing the street when they saw me coming."

At the office where Gladys' husband worked the manager recieved an anonymous letter suggesting he check who in Gladys' family had been arrested for indecent exposure and sexual offenses.

"The answer was no one had," Gladys said, "but it was terribly embarrassing both for my husband and his boss."

Gladys went to the police who promised to investigate.

"They turned up nothing, and we could get no proof who was behind it all," Gladys said. "We had suspicions, but not solid enough to take legal action."

Six months after the hate campaign started, Gladys was heading for a nervous breakdown. She was afraid to answer

54 MAKE YOUR PSYCHIC PYRAMIDIC GENERATOR

the telephone, or even to move far from home, particularly after a dozen rotten eggs were splattered across their neat aluminum siding.

"Having explored all logical avenues, I finally consulted a card reader—one of those ladies who promise to solve all your problems," Gladys said. "Although I know many are fakes, this one was not. She identified the fact that we were being attacked for no good reason, she described three families living in our suburb—but added we would never catch them out in their smear campaign.

"Her advice, which I felt at the time would be totally worthless, was to make a small pyramid and see my enemies defeated by working on South Face routines."

Nothing else had worked, so Gladys duly made a card pyramid and added the symbols as she had been advised.

"I still fail to see any connection between viewing the Fire symbol and the subsequent results," she said, "but our attack ceased. Only normal telephone calls came in. No one threw anything more at the house, our children reported the bullying children no longer used the bus, and our life returned to normal.

"One of the families we suspected watched their uninsured house burn to the ground a week later. Nobody was hurt but they moved to the other side of town.

"The husband in a second family of suspected malefactors was fired from his job and promptly took his wife and dependents far to the East, seeking new work.

"The third family put their home up for sale for no good reason we could discover and resettled a thousand miles away.

"It seems the pyramid caused my enemies to pack up and leave. I'm still startled, but truly grateful."

WHAT TO EXPECT FROM YOUR NEW PSYCHIC ENERGY GENERATOR

What will happen as soon as you build and place your *New Psychic Energy Generator* in its position?

MAKE YOUR PSYCHIC PYRAMIDIC GENERATOR

Visibly, nothing! And that can be a disappointment for some hopeful souls. They perhaps expect a humming and whirring, vibrations, lights, celestial music, a chime of bells and the rustle of angels' wings to announce this start of their journey to a new life.

No such phenomena are likely to occur. Your Generator will just sit there, four square, and nothing you can see or hear will happen. But at the level of the unseen, in the intangible world of luck, emotions, destiny, soul growth, progress and harmony, fantastic events are getting set to happen to you.

From spheres of influence which are as yet still subject to much research, the very forces which shape the future are gearing up to help you. Your part in the equation is to use *New Psychic Energy Power* techniques to indicate what you'd like to happen.

So here come the promised happiness, love, money, luxuries—all in your immediate future the moment you apply the techniques I'm going to explain in subsequent chapters.

JANKE L. STRUCK IT RICH

This case history, a personal experience, illustrates two things. First, that the search for the secrets of Pyramid Power have been going on a long while, and second, some people whom the rest of the world call "strange" use their metaphysical knowledge for vast material gains.

I knew Janke L. more than 15 years ago. That was in the early 60's when bearded hippies were coming on the scene. Janke had looked like a hippie for decades before that!

He use to stride through the town with a pet raven on his shoulder. Janke's clothes should have been deep-sixed years before. Not to put too fine a point on it, both Janke and his garments needed a wash. The pile of raven stuff on his shoulder and down his back bore witness to that, if your nose failed to signal his condition to you first.

He lived in a cave, under deplorable conditions. Nothing

MAKE YOUR PSYCHIC PYRAMIDIC GENERATOR

the local authorities did to him made him change his unsanitary way of life.

Yet he had once been a professor at a famous English school, although he seemed ashamed of that part of his life. His whole existence revolved around Mysticism, Magic and Metaphysics.

"I'm a one-man 3M company," he used to quip, "and one day when I get the hang of the pyramids I'll buy that outfit."

I learned a great deal from Janke in his noisome grotto, with water dripping down the rocks, the fire flaring and smoking and the raven croaking in its sleep.

Janke kept himself fed by prospecting, and despite expert geological evidence which said no gold existed within a hundred miles of his cave, he turned up enough flakes of that valuable metal to satisfy his meager needs.

I met Janke again last year. Rather, he came calling. It caused a bit of local flurry—and I was a mite surprised too—when a bright green helicopter swept in to land on the back acre behind my home.

Out stepped a truly splendid figure. Gold lamé suit, silver boots with diamond buckles. Gems, gold and platinum bejeweled his fingers. He wore a wide-awake hat with a mink band encrusted with emeralds. The fortune in pendants and bangles around his neck should have bowed his shoulders— and might have done so if he had not been so disgustingly healthy!

I did not recognize him. Even his beard was transformed from the old straggling shambles to a neat goatee. Only when he named himself did I realize it was Janke, transformed.

"I finally got the edge on that old pyramid stuff," he called. "Want to tell you about it."

We talked far into the night. He was delighted to share his pyramid discoveries. Much of what he told me is here in this book.

He buzzed off at dawn, heading for his retreat high in the Rockies. During the conversation I had heard of his world

MAKE YOUR PSYCHIC PYRAMIDIC GENERATOR   57

trips, fabulous castles he owns, his highly paid "slaves," his pyramid-shaped house high in the Andes, his gold and treasure expeditions—the whole spectrum of a fantastic way of life.

I do not believe he bought the 3M company as he threatened so long ago. But he could. Mystic turned playboy Janke finally struck it rich!

WHEN YOUR PERSONAL MIRACLES WILL COME TRUE

"I tried one of the methods in your book the same day it arrived. Two days later nothing had happened. What am I doing wrong?"

That statement I read with sorrow in a few of the letters I receive. Similar correspondents ask: "*When* will my personal miracles come true?"

Good questions, and I truly wish there was a single answer which would fit each and every one of my readers. The first question's answer is: "You're doing nothing really wrong. Maybe you're being a mite impatient for openers, but more than that I suspect you've looked up a subject in the index, found the page that attracts you, and used only that page, ignoring the rest of the suggestions in the book."

If I could put this whole method on one page for you, I would—have no doubt about that! However, psychic energy takes a little more explaining and instructing than anything I can pack into about 400 words. What you're holding at this moment is a *complete* self-contained method of applying psychic energy to your life. You may feel you can dip in and take parts of this book without reading and understanding the remainder, and I have to agree that *some* people can do that and achieve success.

But most readers need every word of this book, from the first to the last pages. The ideas and concepts expressed work changes at subconscious levels, and each alteration in your

MAKE YOUR PSYCHIC PYRAMIDIC GENERATOR

thinking patterns prompted by the sentences on these pages is another building block in the whole structure which enables your *New Psychic Energy Power* to flow free and clear to shape coming events to bring you all you could wish for ... and more!

Yes, you're setting yourself up for personal miracles, but you need all the help you can get. Approaching the matter piecemeal reduces your success chances.

And as to when you will finally find yourself surrounded by each and every luxury you can conceive, peaceful, rich, fulfilled by loving companionship, free of pressures, pain and woes for the first time in your life, that again depends on your circumstances.

First, it's a question of priorities. When you come to create your *Akashic List of Desires and Needs* (a psychic tidbit I've reserved for Energy Circuit 11), you'll decide on the right order of things.

Obviously, if you hanker after a full-size pool table, you'll first need to bring yourself a recreation room big enough to put it in! That's a very simple example, but it illustrates how your miracles come step by step, in the right order. You can understand that a pool table delivered to someone who lives in a three-room walk-up would be more a liability than an asset. Instead of bringing pleasure, it would produce turmoil—which is most definitely not the aim of this book.

So the answer to "When?" is this: "Your miracles will occur exactly when the time is right for them to occur for your maximum fulfillment and joy. Some can happen overnight; others will wait in the wings of the future before walking onto your life stage at the precise moment when everything else harmonizes with that miracle."

I'll extend that thought a little with an example, because it's important—especially to those of you who feel that winning a lottery tomorrow, or otherwise getting a large lump sum in cash will give you the peace of mind you desire.

A young acquaintance of mine, a lovely young lady of just 20 years, was sure that $30,000 would solve all her

MAKE YOUR PSYCHIC PYRAMIDIC GENERATOR 59

problems. She had her whole life before her, yet she was so out of tune with harmonious destiny that she was screwing it up badly.

Already she had had an illegitimate child, fathered by a married man she had lived with for a year. She was lonely, her child had been taken from her custody, and she decided that money would solve her loneliness and despair.

What she really needed was a partner to care for her, love her and give her sexual fulfillment. She figured that if she was rich she would automatically attract just such a desirable male.

I'm not aware whether she used psychic methods (if she did, she certainly did not use any that I support), but within a year she had her $30,000 in the bank.

She received the money from an insurance claim: she was involved in an auto accident, broke both legs and suffered painful internal injuries. She was paralyzed for six months, and medical costs over and above her insurance coverage cost her $7,000. The courts awarded her $37,000, which left her with the desired sum.

The money duly brought her the companionship of a male. She lavished her bankroll on him, buying him (among other luxuries) a Harley-Davidson motorbike. Inside of 12 months she had just $800 left, no income, and no prospects of a job. When the money dried up, the boyfriend walked out for good.

Two days later they found what was left of that poor little rich girl in a public park. Alone, unwanted, and again despairing, she had ended her earthly turmoil by blowing her brains out with a handgun.

Yes, she got her money. But no, it did not work miracles for her. She had her priorities wrong: the miracle she needed was a loving companion—then the money could have come, if she felt she still needed it.

That sad real-life example fully answers those of my readers who wonder why their psychic energy fails to win them a lottery the day after they start in on the techniques:

MAKE YOUR PSYCHIC PYRAMIDIC GENERATOR

the time is not yet right—you have to change in some way, or some other miracle must happen first.

And of course the pure joy of this method I'm offering you here is that there's positively no danger of anything drastic happening to you such as what happened to the young lady whose harrowing tale I've just related.

Used as directed in these pages, *New Psychic Energy Power knows* the path to lead you to harmony and peace, and will unerringly do so, bringing changes in the correct order and degree so you're ready to gladly grasp them and handle the results with true cosmic harmony.

MARRIED TO AN ALCOHOLIC, YET LAURA N. SAYS "I'M IN CONTROL"

Laura N.'s case history is a trifle different from the average. She did not aspire to thousands of dollars, a new lover, rejuvenation or any other facets of high living.

Laura's need was simple and clearcut. She loved her husband, Joe, and wanted to be with him and help him. But Joe was an alcoholic.

"Our relationship was breaking up," Laura said. "I rarely wallow in self-pity, but I seemed to be eternally clearing up after him, trying to straighten out our debts and his working hassles, covering up for him. I contacted AA but their counselors said Joe would get well only when *he* decided to stop drinking. They were hopeful but not too helpful.

"I could not get through to Joe. In his rare sober moments he was sorry and guilty, but then he'd slip back and I'd feel that cold despair clutching my heart again. Where would it all end?"

Searching for anything which might help, Laura came across various psychic and mind-power methods, some promising overnight miracles. None of them stopped Joe drinking, no matter how assiduously Laura practiced the chants, techniques, rituals and affirmations.

MAKE YOUR PSYCHIC PYRAMIDIC GENERATOR 61

"After exchanging letters with an author of a psychic self-help book I had a minor revelation," Laura said. "These methods—the genuine ones at least—are exactly that: *self-help*.

"Unless I could get Joe to use mindpower, my efforts would almost certainly fail. So I began working on *myself* to bring peace of mind, acceptance and happiness.

"Joe still drinks. But not as much, and I can see the day when he'll go to AA and quit for good. My own harmony and peace are radiating to him, and giving him strength. I believe we have the problem licked, now that I'm stronger, happier and in control."

HOW DOES YOUR NEW PSYCHIC ENERGY GENERATOR WORK?

Your *New Psychic Energy Generator* is a cosmic apparatus which will change your life. Exactly how it does this is shrouded in mystery. We can talk wisely of vibrations and energies, manipulation of events, shaping the future—but truth to tell we have no more idea of how this all happens than we have of knowing why an apple falls off a tree.

The apple falls because gravity pulls it down. But what gravity *is* has yet to be fathomed by the world's greatest brains.

Similarly, your Generator works miracles in an unseen manner, apparently by focusing the cosmic energy which rules creation. My suggestion to you is to accept evidence which scientists and statisticians would call "empirical." Time after time, when used as suggested, miracles happen to people who employ their *New Psychic Energy Generator.* How it does it remains unknown for now, but the fact that it does indeed work is undeniable.

So use your Generator, literally in good health, and enjoy, enjoy!

62 MAKE YOUR PSYCHIC PYRAMIDIC GENERATOR

LUDOVIC C. NOW KNOWS "WHAT HAPPINESS REALLY IS"

You could call Ludovic C. a student of *New Psychic Energy Power* who earned himself straight A's all across the board. He illustrates how attention to all life aspects with the various techniques brings total fulfillment.

"My existence could not have been described as desperate," Ludovic said, "but it sure was monotonous. A secure job with no chance of anything more than a cost of living raise each year. An affectionate wife, but without any fire of love between us. An average car, a few years old. Some debts, not enough to lie awake over, but just sufficient to put a kink in our plans if we wanted to live a little. A circle of good solid friends, all much like me.

"Some people might envy my security, but I wondered if that was all there was to life. I could see a steady diet of work, a beer or two with the boys, TV sports on Saturday, a brief yearly vacation, then retirement, a rocking chair, and quiet, stagnating end years. Call me ungrateful for wanting to change, but that was not enough for me."

Pyramid techniques pulled Ludovic out of his rut before the sides caved in and stifled him.

"I made a five-year plan," Ludovic said. "I began working steadily on a daily basis at changing the aspects of my life which were fencing me in.

"First I sparked up my energy and natural forces with West Face methods. You should have seen the way our marriage opened up!

"Then I moved into a higher income bracket with North Face work, and once I got moving, I went up and up.

"Minor South Face techniques kept at bay the negativity coming from others who envied the good luck which began raining down on us. Then the East Face ironed out frustrations, brought interesting new people into our circle and instilled a steadiness in me that the world recognizes and responds to.

MAKE YOUR PSYCHIC PYRAMIDIC GENERATOR

"Everything dropped into place as I planned at the outset. Now I'm working on a more ambitious five-year plan. It's fantastic: I now truly know what happiness really is."

EARTH, AIR, FIRE AND WATER SYMBOLS

Having built your *New Psychic Generator* you can add further force to its miraculous abilities by inscribing it with four mystic symbols.

You recall I instructed you to arrange your Generator to face north, south, east and west. The addition I'm suggesting is to add a symbol on each face of your Generator to further focus the forces we're using.

The face to the east is associated with Air; to the west we connect with Water; to the south with Fire; and to the north with Earth.

Figure 3 on this page shows simplified versions of ancient symbols which represent the four elements. Once again, I urge you *not* to cut them out: that's the easy (and useless) way.

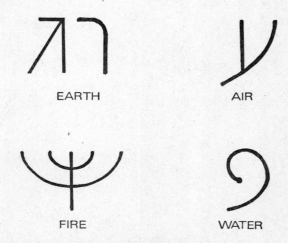

FIGURE 3: Earth, Air, Fire and Water Symbols

MAKE YOUR PSYCHIC PYRAMIDIC GENERATOR

Take the time to draw them onto your Generator, in pencil, felt pen, wax crayon—any writing implement you may have at hand. No need to worry if they're not exactly as shown here: the important thing is that *you* have drawn them, using your hands and mind. If the finished sketches are not quite accurate representations of the symbols in Figure 3, that's fine: they are your personal interpretations of the symbols, tuned to your mind and body.

So add the appropriate symbol on each of the four faces of your Generator and you're another step closer to that ideal life you've only dreamed of so far.

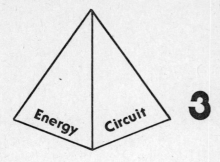

The North Face of Material Wealth

We now begin our tour around the four faces of the pyramid. As we have already noted, the North Face is associated with things you can see and touch, and by tuning yourself in to the energies of this face you automatically bring money, possessions and luxuries into your life.

DEFINING YOUR MATERIAL NEEDS

You'll find as you experience the magnificent aspects of *New Psychic Energy* Power that the guiding principle behind it knows better than you do what is best for your progress and happiness.

You'll notice I emphasize this time after time: you set up the picture of *what* you wish to do, and then let Cosmic Energy decide *how* this will happen. And invariably it occurs in the most natural, harmonious and convenient manner, at the exact time when it will do you the most good.

And here we come to an unusual stumbling block which trips some people. Allow me to remove it immediately!

What stops some of my readers in their tracks is deciding exactly what the word "material" means. As you'll be realizing, we use each face of the pyramid and your *New Psychic Energy Generator* to bring various things to you.

What, then, is strictly "material" and connected with this North Face we're investigating?

If you can see it and touch it, it's material! Anything else—the intangibles like happiness, freedom, health, love, safety and similar concepts—belongs to another face of the pyramid.

Putting that another way, for maximum clarity: if you *can't* touch, see, smell, taste or hear it, then you're not dealing with a material item.

That's an important definition: although the Tides are very flexible and will make allowances for any confusion on your part, you'll find quicker and better results if you can lay down clear ground rules for the Tides to operate within.

And with that clarification behind us, we can move on to bringing all those material advantages which you currently lack and desire. The combined techniques explained here can ensure that you will never again have to worry where the next dollar is coming from.

EDYTHE A. LITERALLY SAILED TO PROSPERITY

Edythe A.'s husband, Wilson, is an invalid. A trucking accident crippled him when he was 23 years old, only six months after Edythe and he had married, hoping to walk happily side by side into the future.

"That was 20 years ago," Edythe said. "We've never been able to have children. But we've had each other, and it's been a true labor of love to care for Wilson.

"I've had to be the breadwinner to add to the disability pension Wilson receives; as prices rose over the years his check has bought less and less."

NORTH FACE OF MATERIAL WEALTH

Edythe and Wilson stuck together through lean times and better times, but life was never easy or leisured.

"I suppose I should be thankful we always survived," Edythe said. "But I began to hanker after a break. Just a single week on a beach with other people to do the chores would have been pure heaven."

Despite every economy, Edythe's attempts to put together a small nest egg were always thwarted. Whenever she had salted away a few dollars, a rise in living costs, a rent hike or an unexpected expense cleaned out her savings.

"A miracle was the only thing that was going to break the vicious circle we were in," Edythe said, "and as my unaided efforts had failed, I began casting around for just such a miracle."

Reading an article in a tabloid newspaper about pyramids and their magic, Edythe wrote to the editorial offices, asking for the address of the man in the story who said he had become wealthy with pyramid power.

"To cut a long story short, I also discovered pyramid miracles," Edythe said. "My need was simple. We already had contentment and love, I was healthy and strong, no one was pressuring us unpleasantly. So I concentrated on North Face Tides.

"My target was to get us a beach cottage where we could spend a weekend or two just taking it easy now and again."

Wilson saw Edythe's pyramid involvement as a harmless diversion. Even today he refuses to get involved with what he calls "those tomfool gizmos." Yet a progressive sequence of events began almost at once for the couple.

"A radio station was running a contest," Edythe said. "I entered, and although I missed the big cash prizes, I won a week's vacation for two at a lakeside resort. That was not quite what I'd envisaged, but we gladly accepted."

During their brief vacation Edythe met the owner of a small fleet of canoes, rowing boats and sailing skiffs. The man ran a profitable summer business, renting the craft to visitors.

"He was getting on in years and was looking for a partner who could take over the business when he retired in a couple of years," Edythe said. "We looked at the options and agreed to give it a try for the rest of the season. We've never looked back since."

Edythe and Wilson have their beach cottage now. Bobbing in front of it is their fleet of brightly colored boats.

"The owner duly retired, we'd made enough to buy him out, and we're joint owners of the business now. I work in the fresh air and sun from May to September, and the rest of the year Wilson and I can relax," Edythe said. "Wilson is getting better since we've been able to afford specialist treatment for him. I always say pyramid power helped us to sail to prosperity!"

MONEY AND POSSESSIONS ARE YOURS WITH THE GOLDEN SQUARE OF PRITHIVI

How would you like to open a door to treasure? Imagine such a door swinging back on its hinges to reveal stacks of dollars, piles of gold pieces, sparkling diamonds, jewelry ... enough wealth to rouse the envy of a fabled sultan!

I'm about to show you such a door, and also reveal your personal key to opening it. And the fascinating feature of this door is that you do not have to move an inch to find it—and *you* decide what material things you wish to find behind it!

This is part of the *North Face of Material Wealth,* and illustrates just one single way of using your *New Psychic Energy Power* to generate your harmony, happiness and riches.

This fabulous "door" to wealth consists simply of a symbol named *the Golden Square of Prithivi*. By placing this symbol in conjunction with your *New Psychic Energy Generator* you achieve a vital attunement with the Cosmic Tides which bring material advantages.

Physically your square consists of a piece of paper, colored gold (or bright yellow). Once again, it's part of the process to create this symbol for yourself, to put you in tune with its unseen powers.

NORTH FACE OF MATERIAL WEALTH

Find a piece of gold foil or yellow paper, and cut a one-inch square from it. If you cannot locate foil or colored paper, use white paper and color it (one side only is fine) with wax crayon, felt pen or any other medium that will turn the paper yellow.

Stand—or rather lean—your completed symbol on edge against the North Face of your *New Psychic Energy Generator*. If there's any danger of your square of yellow paper being blown away by drafts, secure it with a dab of glue or a bit of tape.

Following the next case history, I'll tell you how to make your *Golden Square of Prithivi* become the source of material gains which will amaze you.

"THE FIRST TIME I'VE SEEN MY BANK MANAGER SMILE," SAYS CARL T.

When his employer went bankrupt and closed the doors of his factory, Carl T. joined several hundred others in search of work.

"I was up to my neck in debt at the time," Carl said. "I've never been one to save a dime, and with a job that seemed secure I'd run my credit to the limit.

"When my job folded I added up my liabilities. I was staggered. Charge and credit cards were loaded to the tune of $3,000. I owed the bank $4,000 on my car, and there was over $26,000 still to pay on my house, if I managed to save it from foreclosure. Various utility, food and medical expenses added another $1,000.

"Where was I going to find $34,000 and enough over the top to live on?"

Wisely, Carl went to the bank to explain his position before creditors began getting worried and taking legal or collection action.

"I guess they were polite, but not exactly overjoyed to hear my story," Carl said. "After some figuring, the manager told me the only way I could prevent myself following my employer into insolvency was either to come up with about $5,000 within 90 days or to find a spare $10,000 a year for the next five years.

"That was just to clear the debts; food, clothing and other living expenses would be over and above those figures."

When all else fails, try psychic energy. Carl says that was the decision he arrived at in the following days. No work showed up, the mail brought more requests for money, the telephone became a nightmare—"Mr. T., *when* can we expect an installment...?" —and Carl entertained several insistent callers at his home with coffee and empty promises.

"I'd known about pyramids and the *Golden Square of Prithivi* for a while, but treated them as a joke," Carl said. "A friend of mine who retired to Florida after a legacy made him filthy rich swore that the Golden Square had set it up for him.

"I thought I was more practical than that, figuring to be above such kookiness. But I was soon prepared to try anything once, and more than once if I liked it!"

Carl's *Golden Square of Prithivi* did not bring him an inheritance.

"Better than that," Carl said. "I've always been a bit of an inventor and ten years ago I made and patented an electrical generator for home use. No one wanted to back it at the time, I lacked the funds to develop it, so I let it slip into the past."

On the tenth day after he began his daily Golden Square routine with his pyramid, Carl was contacted by an industrialist who was exploiting the energy shortage by creating new sources of energy. Search of the patent office had turned up Carl's invention of so long ago.

"I sold the rights in a package deal," Carl said. "Up front was a check for $100,000 and I signed a contract to collect a 10% royalty off each unit manufactured. The first quarterly payment to me was over $15,000, and sales are expanding.

"No more money worries for me. The *Golden Square of Prithivi* started something for me, and one of the best spin-

NORTH FACE OF MATERIAL WEALTH

offs happened when I deposited that first check. It's the very first time I've seen my bank manager smile!"

CREATE INSTANT ASSETS WITH THE NEW PSYCHIC ENERGY IMAGE TECHNIQUE

You're about to really start making Cosmic Energy work for you. This simple technique increases the "tuning in" process I've been talking about.

Your *New Psychic Energy Generator* and the *Golden Square of Prithivi* are the link between your material world and the unseen world where destiny arranges what is going to happen to whom. By slipping mentally into tune with the North Face Tide, you make certain that your share of the future is loaded with all the material assets you could possibly need—and then some!

Schedule a few moments of your day so you can sit comfortably and look at the North Face of your *New Psychic Energy Generator.* As you sit and view the yellow square, relax and consider what your material needs are. Close your eyes for a few moments and think about what you desire destiny to bring you in the material sense.

Worry not *how* it will come; no matter how desperate your condition, how hopeless life seems, it's destiny's job to turn that around and bring you everything you need. Your simple task is to strongly entertain thoughts of the physical items you wish to be around you.

Do your best to make your thoughts powerful: for example, if it's dollar bills you're seeking, think about their color, their shape, how they feel, how they smell.

But also be quite sure it's money you really require. When you get the cash, what are you going to do with it? Pay off bills, perhaps. So as part of this technique, instead of aiming for the money alone, go the whole way to the destined end of the process: revel in the idea that all your bills have been paid. In your mind, see the cancelled accounts, with a big fat "PAID IN FULL" stamped on all of them.

72   NORTH FACE OF MATERIAL WEALTH

Maybe it's a new car you intend to bring with the money you're tuning in to. So think about that car: how it will feel as you sit behind the wheel, its design, name, color, model, options ... as many details as you can mentally conjure up.

Whatever it is you need, exert your thoughts and mental powers to imagine what it will be like when your desire has been fulfilled. For a few moments, do your level best to convince yourself that it has already happened.

And having run those thoughts through your mind as strongly as you know how, open your eyes again and view the *Golden Square of Prithivi* for a few more seconds before you stand up and carry on with your daily routines.

LOLA V. HAD A WAD OF HUNDRED-DOLLAR BILLS FALL AT HER FEET

Pyramid energy specializes in turning the impossible into reality, but sometimes its instant response is so incredible as to boggle the mind.

I'll grant I myself was skeptical when I was told the following case history until I checked with unimpeachable witnesses and found it to be factual.

Lola V. is an avid California Pyramid Energy user who firmly believes that the Great Pyramid of Gizeh contains all the secrets of the Universe.

"I've conducted many experiments with pyramids," she said, "and met with both successes and failures as I researched. My most amazing success came with the *Golden Square of Prithivi*.

"I had set a target of $5,000 as a desire. The object of the exercise was not to have money to spend but to see if the miracle would work. If I got the cash I would give it to charity."

Lola set up the Golden Square one morning and went downtown the same afternoon.

NORTH FACE OF MATERIAL WEALTH

"I was passing a store when a man came sprinting out of a door clutching a leather satchel under his arm," Lola related. "Two men were chasing him, yelling their heads off.

"Across the sidewalk was a powerful car, engine roaring and a door swinging open. The running man was heading for it, and was going to make a clean getaway if no one stopped him."

Without stopping to think, Lola thrust her umbrella between the man's legs as he brushed past her.

"He went down in a heap, the satchel went up in the air, fell to the sidewalk and burst open. Money cascaded out, and a thick wad of hundred-dollar bills fell right at my feet," Lola said. "The pursuers fell on the fallen thief, picked up the cash with my help, had police chase and apprehend the accomplice in the car, and everything quieted down.

"It had all happened so quick I had no time to be scared."

The upshot of her adventure was that Lola was rewarded. The man had snatched the money from the accounts department of the store as they were getting it ready for the bank, and if Lola had not intervened the store would have been some $100,000 poorer.

"I was feted and praised for my heroism, my picture was in the paper, and the manager of the store publicly handed me a check for $5,000," Lola said. "That went straight to cancer research as I'd intended. My joy was to see the *Golden Square of Prithivi* prove its powers so immediately and convincingly."

SPARK UP YOUR MUNDANE LIFE WITH THE NORTHERN EARTH APPLICATION

Next time you're out in your yard, someone else's yard or a park, pick up a pinch of earth and take it home with you.

Put a few grains of this soil beside the North Face of your *New Psychic Energy Generator*. Even better, sprinkle a little of the earth on the sticky side of an inch-long piece of tape and adhere it to the North Face.

That small and simple gesture ties a further bond between you and the Earth vibrations of the North Face Tide, and adds strength to the attunement process with your *Golden Square of Prithivi.*

MONOTONY "FLEW OUT OF THE WINDOW" FOR LUCKY PHIL K.

Phil K. is yet another Pyramid Energy user who attests to the miraculous events which follow when anyone tunes in to those unseen Tides.

"Whenever I need something extra to make life more stimulating I set up my *New Psychic Energy Generator* and gaze on the *Golden Square of Prithivi,*" Phil said. "It rarely fails, and I've conclusively proved to myself that the addition of earth to the North Face adds more zap to the powers and processes."

Phil's most memorable pyramid effort came just after he added the *Northern Earth Application* to his regular techniques.

"I desired a new car," he said, "one with everything. A fully-loaded Stingray in iridescent gold."

Using the precise method described above, Phil poured his heart and soul into the process.

"While I sat there I pretended I was charging my new wheels around a racetrack at 140," he said. "I imagined the purr of the engine, the rush of wind muffled by the music from the quadrophonic tape deck. I thought about the vibrating power of the quivering wheel under my hands, the controls under my feet, with the concrete unreeling before me, seen through the tinted glass surrounded by gleaming chrome.

"Within a week a friend who needed money offered me ... you've guessed it! ... his iridescent gold Stingray at a ridiculous price. I owned it for a while until the novelty wore off, then sold it for $1,000 more than I paid for it.

NORTH FACE OF MATERIAL WEALTH

75

"Life is incredibly interesting since I took up with Pyramid Energy. Everything I desire is in my Generator, and as soon as I picture it, along it comes. Monotony flew out of the window for me when I discovered *New Psychic Energy Power*."

BANISH NEW DEBTS FOREVER WITH THE GLACIAL RING-PASS-NOT

One of the more worrisome aspects of this modern life is the depressing frequency with which debts can accumulate. In addition to existing liabilities, it's all too easy to acquire new liabilities. The month-end pile of accounts can become a mountain of despair which grows ever larger no matter how hard you battle to stay ahead.

Even the "magic" of consolidation promised by some financial organizations often changes things only from many separate aggravations into a single crippling monthly burden.

Solution? Well, for openers you could try the *Glacial Ring-Pass-Not,* designed to prevent more debts from piling up. Many users of this technique say it provides a miraculous bulwark against going deeper in debt.

Miraculous, yes—but please note that stated purpose of the Ring-Pass-Not: it's designed to be used with other techniques if you wish to get *out* of debt. The Ring-Pass-Not merely prevents new debts being piled onto an already overloaded income.

You should consider this to be a powerful deterrent which holds the line for you while you call on other methods to clean up the financial mess you've gotten yourself into.

The *Glacial Ring-Pass-Not* works at deep mental and spiritual levels to bring results in the material world. While you're applying any of the other North Face techniques and processes, take the time to gather together all the unpaid bills, demand notes, statements and other physical evidence of your need to balance your budget more efficiently.

76   *NORTH FACE OF MATERIAL WEALTH*

Create the *Glacial Ring-Pass-Not* in this manner. Look at the debt papers, and pretend a cool rain-laden breeze is blowing across them. If it's necessary to your visualization, blow gently at the papers to make them move a trifle.

Now pretend a shower of freezing rain is soaking the papers, encasing them in frost and gradually setting them firmly inside a block of ice.

If you have trouble imagining what that would look like, you could actually freeze a piece of scrap paper as an example. Float any old piece of paper in a saucer of water and leave it in the freezer section of your refrigerator overnight. Next morning your saucer will contain an example of what I'm suggesting you visualize with the application of the *Glacial Ring-Pass-Not.*

When you have the idea of the frozen bills firmly in mind, turn your gaze on the *Golden Square of Prithivi* for about half a minute, and then return to your regular household routines.

Childish pretense? So it may seem, yet it works. Many people tell me that such visualization literally "freezes" their debts and prevents the sum from growing larger.

"IN THE BLACK FOR THE FIRST TIME I CAN RECALL," WRITES DOROTHY M.

"My marriage got off on the wrong foot," wrote Dorothy M. "We bought everything on time, so we owned nothing and owed everything.

"The strain of keeping up payments chipped away at our newly wed adjustment to each other. We had heated arguments when Bill, my husband, had a night out with the boys, while I took my lumps from him if I dared to buy a new pair of shoes. Our overdraft grew as our mutual respect grew less."

Three years of hand-to-mouth existence, bad luck with employers and unexpected medical expenses found Dorothy and Bill barely tolerating each other, going deeper in the hole each week.

NORTH FACE OF MATERIAL WEALTH

"First we fought to pay the bills, then we fought each other," Dorothy said. "We separated when neither of us could stand the strain any longer. I was saddled with almost half our debts, with two young children to care for into the bargain."

While talking to the lawyer who was arranging the terms of the separation, Dorothy was intrigued by a small home-made pyramid the lawyer kept on his desk.

"I tell my colleagues it's merely a keepsake," the lawyer told Dorothy, "but that's only to conceal the fact that I firmly believe Pyramid Energy keeps me solvent and successful."

If a logical lawyer could use pyramid power, Dorothy figured she might give it a try, even though the whole idea was strange to her.

"The lawyer said I was typical of people who needed to practice what he called the *Glacial Ring-Pass-Not*," Dorothy related. "It sounded to me like a restaurant dessert, but I took his instructions for building and using a *New Psychic Energy Generator*."

Dorothy is still wondering how it worked, but work it did.

"Sure enough, although I still had doubts, my total of debts stayed steady after using the *Glacial Ring-Pass-Not*," she related. "With the addition of other *New Psychic Energy Power* techniques I pulled myself out of trouble."

The postscript to this case history comes from a letter Dorothy wrote to a friend, describing her experiences with *New Psychic Energy Power*. "I was not one of those who saw an overnight miracle of troubles vanishing like magic. Just a feeling of certainty everything would turn out fine. It took a while, but I finally got my bank balance into the black—for the first time I can recall!

"Did you know I'd remarried? To whom? Why, to Ken, the lawyer who introduced me to *New Psychic Energy Power* in the first place. Seems he was using East Face techniques to find a suitable wife, and along I came, filling the bill precisely!"

NORTH FACE OF MATERIAL WEALTH

IMPROVE YOUR GAMBLING LUCK WITH THE AMAZING TRIAD ATTUNEMENT

Before we get to this amazing piece of Cosmic attunement, please attend closely to the following.

I know from experience that many of my readers believe that the *only* way they can leave a life of hopelessness, debt and despair is to win big on a lottery. So their first impulse when they get their hands on a book such as this one is to turn to techniques for winning the lottery or beating the horses.

This works for *some* people ... but most definitely not for *all*. Relying on its working for you *personally,* quickly, can be disappointing. Winning a lottery (or coming out ahead in any other form of gambling) depends on catching destiny in a positive swing when you buy your ticket or when the gamble is made.

How do you know when such positive swings of destiny occur for you? If I knew the precise answer to that I'd gladly tell you, and all the casinos would go broke. What I *can* tell you is that it's easy to see when destiny is *not* swinging your way, and at such times you're very unlikely to win at any kind of chance.

If you're in trouble, you're into a low swing of destiny's effects on you. Within the concepts of this book, we can say you're out of phase with the Tides of the Cosmos, and need to apply the techniques designed to get you back into positive line with such Tides. Fighting against the Tides brings "bad luck," turmoil, pain and lack of progress—so if you're suffering from any of those, by definition you're not in a position to be able to hope for a lottery win.

Have I made that crystal clear? I certainly hope so, because what I'm proposing to you is that *before* you start trying to win at gambling, you should straighten out other areas of your life, and get those into harmonious shape. Once you've done that you'll at least know that you're riding with a

NORTH FACE OF MATERIAL WEALTH

positive Tide of Destiny, so you've improved your chances of winning.

And by adding the *Amazing Triad Attunement,* you (like many others before you) could get to be ultimately lucky—provided you do it at the right time. And that right time, as I've carefully explained, is *after* you've put yourself into a more progressive phase with the Cosmic Tides.

Performing this small mental ritual is simplicity itself. Conditions are the same as for viewing the *Golden Square of Prithivi.* Look at the Square, then turn your attention to the top point of your *New Psychic Energy Generator.* Pretend you're standing up there, with the Golden Square sloping down *below* you. Then along the north base edge of your Generator, in you mind's eye, see all the people you're competing against when you gamble. Got that picture? You stand at the apex, with the rest of the world down below.

That's the picture to hold in your mind for a few seconds. Then go out and buy your lottery ticket or whatever—but *only* when you know you've turned the corner towards riding with, not against, the Tides of the Cosmos. That evidence is shown by improvements occurring in the quality of your life: if you gamble before you see such positive changes, you're pouring good money down the drain.

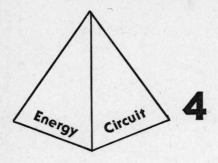

The East Face of Love and Peace of Mind

Moving right around from the material rewards which come from the North Face, we now regard the East Face, identified with the ecstatic intangibles of love and peace of mind.

Before you figure you cannot put such things in the bank, and decide to skip this Energy Circuit, hold on one minute. Whether you realize it or not, you *need* love and peace before you can hope to enjoy life as your Creator intended you to. And when I use the word "love" I do not necessarily imply sex, or the pure carnality which is promoted so prominently on some newsstands these days.

In a more general sense than the skin-mags portray, you need love. Even if you're a hermit with little or no contact with other people, one person you need to love is *yourself.* The way you see yourself as a person is often the way the rest of the world sees you also. So if you do not like the person you are, it's likely that destiny will also seem to be at odds with you: others get the breaks while luck leaves you on the sidelines.

That's a facet of love you may not have thought about,

EAST FACE OF LOVE AND PEACE OF MIND

but it's all part of the gloriously fulfilling bonuses the East Face Tide can bring you, once you turn yourself around and swim with the Tide instead of against it.

DECIDE ON YOUR LOVE DESIRES AND THEY'RE YOURS

Just as we defined the word "material" when we were exploring the North Face, so we now need to decide what the word "love" means to you. More important, you need to decide what parts of this overall idea of love are missing from your life, so you can have the partial picture completed and thus find true satisfaction and joy.

And please do not neglect the second vital aspect of the East Face: as well as fleshing out your love desires to their limit, the even more tenuous—but infinitely precious—attribute of peace of mind is yours when you are aligned with the East Face Tide.

However, most people who wish to use the powers of the East Face automatically think of attracting a partner. With loneliness on the increase in every stratum of modern society, that's hardly surprising—the human animal has a basic need to share, to jointly experience and, of course, to procreate.

The East Face Tide has all you could want of those for you. All you need to do is decide what love and peace of mind means to you, and it's yours. The only conditions under which the East Face Tide will fail to comply with your wishes is when your love aims would ultimately bring less harmony and satisfaction than you anticipate. Once again, you'll see the Tides and Cosmic Energy illustrating their principle that destiny knows better than you do what will be best for you. Your short-term picture of satisfaction may not be one which leads to long-lasting peace and fulfillment.

So when you begin your East Face techniques, give the Tide some latitude. By that I mean try not to insist on too many minor details (especially physical ones), otherwise the

82   *EAST FACE OF LOVE AND PEACE OF MIND*

Tide will use much energy (and therefore time) to fulfill your desires.

An example will serve to illustrate that point. Jim K., a late-40's bachelor I knew, used the East Face techniques to improve his then-monotonous lovelife. As well as seeking a loving and fulfilling companion, Jim also fed in his own idea of a perfect lover: his visualization included a petite, blue-eyed, scantily clad, perfectly proportioned lady.

Within a year he was very happily married to an ideal wife, yet she hardly resembled the "perfect lover" fantasy Jim had been nursing. He used to joke with me about it—until two years after he entered the marital state. At that time the couple had a baby, which made their mutual joy supreme.

"Peace of mind, joy and happiness," Jim said. "It all came true with the harmony of the East Face Tide. And the baby added that final touch of perfection and togetherness. It took me quite a while to realize that Cosmic Energy had finally completed the picture I'd set up three years before ... I had indeed been brought a tiny, blue-eyed lady!"

Yes, the East Face Tide will assuredly bring your desires to pass—but if you insist on every detail being in accord with your conscious ideas, it may take some time for the picture to become complete in the material plane.

"I FOUND MY PERSONAL HAREM," SAYS AHMED N.

This case history aptly illustrates how Cosmic Energy swept into action for an individual who applied East Face techniques and brought himself harmonious results.

"Let's face it, my favorite reading matter was *Playboy* and similar magazines," Ahmed N. said. "I nursed the same fantasies as many other males, and the 'bunnies' represented my highest ideal in seeking a love partner.

"But I've never been one to bowl the girls over with good

EAST FACE OF LOVE AND PEACE OF MIND

looks or a sparkling personality. Even after I outgrew my teenage acne I had precious little to offer in the shape of sleek cars, high-on-the-hog living or jetset goings-on."

The facts were simple: Ahmed's parents had immigrated from India; his father ran a store in an Eastern city; and the family lived in a neighborhood which, although friendly and comfortable, was not renowned for opulence.

Ahmed worked on the gas pumps at a garage and rarely had much money to spend on pleasure. Most of his spare time he spent studying to gain an engineering diploma.

"I was also painfully shy, and missed out on having a regular girlfriend," he said. "By the time I was 25 my parents were wondering out loud when I would marry. Most people seemed to consider me the area's least eligible bachelor."

In the course of his studies and leisure reading Ahmed read various books on Pyramid Energy which caught his attention.

"The data on the East Face, where you could tune in to love, fascinated me," he said. "I guess it was something of a sly personal joke, but I dreamed up a fantastic partner who would satisfy my every need and whim. Then, more in hope than any kind of firm expectation, I tried the East Face Tide routines."

It took the Tide less than a month to work on Ahmed's request and bring results.

"It was amazing. All I had to do was go along with events," Ahmed said. "The sister of a guy I work with dropped by the garage to have her coupe serviced. Something went *bing!* between us, we started dating, and were married within six months of our first meeting.

"Our love nest is everything I ever dreamed about. My wife is a perfect hostess at home, a whiz in the kitchen, an ideal companion when we go out—and if I were a poet, I might try to describe what she is in the bedroom. Let's just put it that the East Face Tide brought me my personal harem and geisha girl rolled into one!"

84　EAST FACE OF LOVE AND PEACE OF MIND

AUTOMATIC FREEDOM FROM DESPAIR
WITH THE BLUE CIRCLE OF VAYU

The five techniques associated with the East Face are carefully graded. All lead to their promised target, but you'll notice their different approaches. You choose the one which best fits your personal conditions and needs, moving on to another technique as soon as the desirable changes have taken place.

This first technique has a very broad aim. Its purpose is to remove personal attitudes which can *cause* lack of love and peace of mind.

This is neither a psychological nor a psychiatric treatise, so we need not investigate the complexes which make one person attractive and another unattractive to others. We will simply say that if you're not attracting the people and conditions you desire, part of the problem is within yourself.

One source of unattractiveness is personal despair, where you are locked into a circle of negative emotions which feeds on itself. You've fought to be accepted and liked, failed, and retired emotionally hurt, convinced the world hates you. That kind of firm idea can, because of the attitude you radiate, become an actual reality.

The *Blue Circle of Vayu* is designed to reverse the effects of any such emotional spiral, as the symbol works on deep levels of your subconscious mind.

Just as you did with the *Golden Square of Prithivi*, you're going to create a symbol which you use with your *New Psychic Energy Generator* to attune yourself with Cosmic Tides.

Your circle is made from a piece of blue paper. Draw a circle about one inch across on your paper. The *exact* size is unimportant and the exact shade of blue depends on your personal preference. Laying a quarter on the paper and running a pencil around it will produce a circle about the right size, and if you have several shades of blue to consider, use the one you like best. And, of course, if you cannot find a piece

EAST FACE OF LOVE AND PEACE OF MIND

of blue paper, use a white piece and color it blue with ink, crayon or paint.

Cut out your circle, and lean it against the East Face of your *New Psychic Energy Generator*. Stick it to the Generator with gum or tape if you're worried about its blowing away.

You have now personally created another link to the unseen realms of destiny, this time connecting you to the abstract world of emotions.

To start your basic tuning in to the world of emotional peace and attraction, set up conditions similar to those you set up for viewing the *Yellow Square of Prithivi*. The difference is that you arrange your seat so you can look at the *East* Face of your *New Psychic Energy Generator*.

Look steadily at the Blue Circle for a couple of minutes, then gently allow your eyes to close. Under some lighting conditions you will see an image of the circle floating against the darkness of your eyelids. Whether or not you see this is not critical: I mention it only as a point of interest and because someone is sure to ask why it happens. It's a purely physical phenomenon and occurs because the retina of the eye gets "tired" of looking at the color. It's neither dangerous to your sight nor significant to your psychic path.

Unlike the Yellow Square technique, this time there's no need to exercise your mind at visualizing your needs. What we're doing here is simple strengthening your attunement with the *East Face Tide of Harmony and Peace*.

If you should find your mind galloping along a mile a minute as you close your eyes, with worries and troubles tumbling over each other for attention, push them into the background for the moment. Think instead of a calm and happy incident in your life; think about quiet places, peaceful surroundings—the deep woods at dawn, for instance, or the holy quiet of a grand cathedral.

You'll feel some of that peace begin to spread through your being at once. Naturally, how much immediate effect the *Blue Circle of Vayu* has depends on exactly how uptight and desperate you are at the outset. But a couple of minutes a day

86 *EAST FACE OF LOVE AND PEACE OF MIND*

(or as often as feasible on a less regular basis) spent contemplating the Blue Circle will assuredly work fabulous changes in your outlook.

Keep your eyes closed for another couple of minutes, then open them. View the Blue Circle for about half a minute longer, then stand up and continue with whatever else needs doing in your life.

CAROL Y. MET MR. RIGHT AFTER YEARS OF MISERY

Carol Y. spent many of her adult waking hours in a haze of tranquilizer-induced fogginess. At age 10 she had been sexually assaulted by a psychotic male, and the experience had left her with deep-seated mental scars.

"I was scared of men," she said. "Even 20 years later, applying logic and adult perspective to that terrifying childhood experience, I could not relate comfortably to anyone of the opposite sex.

"I found myself freezing up or becoming bitterly vocal whenever a man began to get close to me. That wrecked any hope of my achieving a fulfilling lovelife, and even made me strained and nervous in employment situations."

Despite therapy, Carol's condition remained disturbing. Her doctor finally prescribed tranquilizers to dull her response to her subconscious fears, in the hope she would eventually adjust to normal relationships.

"I find it difficult to describe the frustrations of my emotional state," she said. "On the one hand I was reasonably attractive with the normal needs of any young woman. I had no problem attracting males who would have been pleased to be prospective partners.

"Yet no matter how I fought with myself, I withdrew from them all. My reactions ranged from insane laughter to loud and angry verbal responses, and that turned off boyfriends long before we could reach a meaningful level of interchange."

EAST FACE OF LOVE AND PEACE OF MIND 87

Eventually Carol had cut herself off from all contact with males except for unavoidable routine meetings in her daily life.

"Only someone who felt the way I did could even start to understand my misery," she said. "I could not come to terms with being condemned to spinsterhood because of that long-ago trauma.

"I had a small circle of female acquaintances but I was seen as an awkward friend by them: I fell apart if they happened to have their husbands with them when we met."

Casting around for a cure, Carol tried various meditation and psychic mind techniques which looked promising.

"Nothing worked very efficiently until I was introduced to Pyramid Energy," she said. "Learning about the *East Tide of Harmony and Peace* was followed by incredible improvements in my emotional outlook.

"I had merely hoped for peace of mind to accept my own psychology and to come to terms with the problem and perhaps be able to give up the tranquilizers. I never expected a total cure."

Carol found a daily viewing of the *Blue Circle of Vayu* brought a pronounced calming effect.

"I knew I'd turned the corner when I found myself smiling at the bus driver when I paid my fare," she said. "Previously even that minor transaction had caused me palpitations and withdrawal."

Carol's path to mental health opened up rapidly. She was able to abandon the pills, and she was soon dating regularly with several males.

"Then along came Ben, a photographer," she said. "He was everything I'd ever wanted in a man, and now I was able to reach out to him. He was gentle and understanding, and our relationship quickly bloomed into true love and mutual esteem."

Today Carol is married to Ben. They have a fine home in Michigan, three lovely and lively children, and a relationship which is the envy of their friends.

EAST FACE OF LOVE AND PEACE OF...

"It was truly worth waiting for," Carol said, "and
never have happened without the *East Face Tide* sho
the way."

DISPEL LONELINESS WITH THE MAGNETIC
PICTORIAL TECHNIQUE

Now we move a step closer to specifics. The Blue Circle
technique previously described was designed to bring peace
and harmony with no special aim in view. This extension of
the method is designed to cure the conditions of those who
feel lonely and unwanted.

You need a picture or a photograph for this stage of your
attunement. From a newspaper or magazine, cut a picture of
a person who is looking happy and friendly. You'll find one of
the models posing in many advertisements fits the bill
admirably.

The picture you use needs to be of a stranger, so do *not*
use a photograph of an ex-lover, relative, or anyone else
connected with your life.

The sex of the person in the picture is not important: the
factor you need in the person you're going to look at is radiant
happiness and warmth.

Carry out the steady viewing of the *Blue Circle of Vayu*
as I previously described for you, but before you close your
eyes, turn your gaze on the picture you've selected. Attend to
the person's face: look at the curve of the lips, the facial
expression, and particularly the eyes.

After a minute or so of this examination, allow your own
eyes to close as before.

Again push away worries or troubles, this time by
pretending you're walking along a path in warm sunshine,
heading toward a city on a hill. Beside you is a companion,
radiating warmth, friendliness and happiness.

Practice that for a full minute (or longer if you wish),
open your eyes, and end the exercise just as you did the
previous viewing of the Blue Circle.

EAST FACE OF LOVE AND PEACE OF MIND

Another link is firmly forged in your chain connecting you to ultimate peace of mind. The *Magnetic Pictorial Technique* you've now entertained is duly registered in the book of destiny and will assuredly come true for you as you keep practicing this every day, or whenever it is convenient for you to do so.

ELWOOD R. NOW HAS "MORE FRIENDS THAN I KNOW WHAT DO DO WITH"

Moing into the big city did wonders for Elwood R.'s bank account but it wrecked his social life.

"I was raised in a small Iowa town where everyone knew everyone else," he said. "People were naturally friendly, and I never had any problem finding friends to share my leisure time.

"Trouble was, when I left school I had too many spare hours. I was not anxious to work on my father's farm, and local job opportunities were not exactly copious. After a couple of years at carhopping, snack bar waiting and similar 'no future' work, I decided I'd have to move away to do better than that."

Elwood relocated to Los Angeles and worked hard at establishing himself. Always a good student, he gained a diploma in electronics and was soon making good money and advancing steadily as a technician with an organization manufacturing semiconductor devices.

"I was much happier," he said. "I was able to rent and furnish a good apartment, buy a reasonable car and surround myself with all the signs of the good life of a young bachelor.

"Only trouble was I had no one to enjoy it with. I'd made no social connections worth a plugged nickel. My workmates were mostly married or getting ready to be, and while I'd been poring over my books I'd never opened up to making friends. Consequently I was seen as a loner, and in typical city style, people left me alone to do my own thing."

EAST FACE OF LOVE AND PEACE OF MIND

Fate would not cooperate with Elwood's efforts to find worthwhile friends.

"I went to singles bars, discos and other clubs, yet nothing clicked. The types I met were either not for me, or they were transients who passed out of my life within hours or days," Elwood said. "I used to sit listening to my stereo recalling happy times past, when life was easy and unhurried in the country. I was sorely tempted to go back to that until I realized I'd have to give up a great deal I had worked hard for.

"The absence of true friends was the only fly in the ointment. The rest of my existence was pretty good."

Scanning the classifieds for ads which could lead him to meet people, Elwood noted a group of people who were looking for interested contacts "to experiment with psychic and occult disciplines."

As a pragmatic person to whom one and one always had to make two, Elwood had never been much interested in such subjects.

"Sure I scanned my astrology sign in the papers. I knew about ESP, telepathy and suchlike. But from the little I knew on the subjects I considered them to be a mixture of unscientific investigation and over-enthusiasm," he said. "Certainly I had never thought of any of those methods as useful in daily life for problem-solving."

Elwood met the group of psychic researchers and even then was not over-impressed.

"They formed a discussion group meeting weekly," he said. "I heard of many subjects I'd never before encountered, and Pyramid Energy caught my attention. I found a great deal of true scientific research had been done on it, mostly with inconclusive results. But I figured if universities could spend good money on electronic mapping of the Great Pyramid[1] there must be something in it.

[1] In 1972 scientists abandoned a program intended to map hidden chambers in the Great Pyramid of Gizeh. Patterns of received radiation within the structure altered inexplicably. Radar research by Stanford Research Institute was also interrupted in 1974 when equally anomalous results were obtained.

EAST FACE OF LOVE AND PEACE OF MIND   **91**

"With true scientific detachment and anticipating negative results I faithfully carried out the allocated *Magnetic Pictorial Technique*," he said. "My notes taken at the time witness a record of success that I still find unbelievable.

"Within a couple of weeks the phone began ringing off the wall with invitations to parties, beach outings and sea cruises. A whole new world of delightful social involvement opened up for me. I can truly say I now have more friends than I know what to do with! I'm thankful I was able to prove the powers of the *Blue Circle of Vayu*."

BRING A PERFECT LOVER WITH THE
EASTERN AIR TECHNIQUE

"Unrequited" is the word. Hundreds—nay, thousands—of people in today's world are unsatisfied with their lovelife. Despite all the TV and newspaper ads which promise that this deodorant, wine, toothpaste, mouthwash, pill, product or whatever will bring a lover to your side, many people are desperately seeking their ideal lover, the perfect person who is in harmony at spiritual, mental and physical levels.

Are you one of those folk? If so, the *Eastern Air Technique* is for you, in a further aspect of the power of the *Blue Circle of Vayu.*

A perfect lover is your need, someone to cherish and adore you, stimulate you, laugh, cry, work and play with you. So shall it be—if you'll let the East Face Tide do the work, and do not insist on details which may *seem* important to you, but are merely surface, material appearances.

I know that many readers entertain a picture of their favorite movie star or C&W singer as their perfect lover. That may be fine for erotic fantasies, but for-the-rest-of-your-life love is likely to be a mite different from your sexual-fulfillment dreams. The achievement of love and harmony is much more than two people being physically suited—and the East Face

92 EAST FACE OF LOVE AND PEACE OF MIND

Tide will take *all* factors into consideration when bringing you a compatible companion.

The process, simple in essence, brings powerful forces to bear at inner levels of existence where your future is being formulated, and you insert the powers of the *Blue Circle of Vayu* and the *Air Symbol* into the equation to assure a favorable outcome when the time is right.

Carry out your observation of the *Blue Circle of Vayu* as if you are performing the *Magnetic Pictorial Technique*. But in place of the picture you were instructed to study for that technique, during this one substitute a small sketch of the *Air Symbol,* copied onto a piece of paper as you did when you inscribed the East Face of your *New Psychic Energy Generator.*

Try to engrave the shape of the Air Symbol on your mind and memory. Examine it closely so that at any time in the future you can recall its curves and shape, somewhat like a cursive letter "Y."

Having fixed this symbol in your conscious mind, close your eyes for a full minute, still continuing to think about the symbol. Then open your eyes and end this exercise by gazing at the *Blue Circle of Vayu* as previously instructed.

The results of this exercise depend partly upon what you do thereafter. Carry your Air Symbol with you in your purse or wallet, and be alert for all chances to meet the perfect lover who is now in your future.

Destiny welcomes initiative. You *could* sit at home and wait for your new love to phone, or to come knocking at your door. That's been known to work for a few people, but a far better plan is to place yourself in areas where you're likely to meet a responsive and compatible partner. In essence, the more variety and movement you voluntarily put into your life, the more you're inviting quick results.

Note Emily G.'s success in the following case history, and emulate her.

EAST FACE OF LOVE AND PEACE OF MIND

"HE'S JUST WHAT I'VE ALWAYS DREAMED ABOUT," SAYS EMILY G.

Nine years and three disastrous marriages convinced Emily G. she was doomed to accepting third-best and worse in her love relationships.

She had just gone through the disruption of her third divorce and had hit bottom emotionally.

"I had this raw certainty that Cupid used poison darts on my heart," she said. "Every man I had known had turned out to be a lush, a cheater or a monster. Better I should not go into the sordid details, but married life had been several varieties of Hades for me."

Strongly encouraged by a sympathetic friend, Emily hopelessly took up with Pyramid Energy which her friend assured her offered a ray of hope in her turmoil.

"My friend told me how her own fulfillment had increased a hundred per cent with the *Eastern Air Technique,*" Emily said. "I told her it might work for her, but I was beyond hope, almost as if I'd been cursed. But to please someone who was going out of her way to try to help me, I agreed to practice it.

"It was something different to do other than moping around the house with sad memories as my only company."

The glad and sudden changes in Emily's emotional experiences make her a classic example of how Pyramid Energy can work miracles for some within days.

"I performed the *Eastern Air Technique* on a Friday evening, and again on Saturday and Sunday," Emily relates. "I tucked the Air Symbol in my purse and took it to work with me on Monday."

That same day a new manager was appointed to the credit department of the large store where Emily worked.

"He came around introducing himself to each of his staff, stopping to talk a short while with everyone," Emily

94   EAST FACE OF LOVE AND PEACE OF MIND

said. "I'm afraid I behaved like a school kid when he spoke to me. I blushed and actually giggled—he was the type of man I'd always fantasized. But knowing my track record in the game of love I held out no hopes of anything."

Yet during the week the new boss singled Emily out for attention. First it seemed to be routine errands which brought her into his office, but before the end of the week they were taking coffee breaks together.

"He asked me if I'd enjoy an evening on the town at the weekend," Emily remembers. "Would I ever! It was perfectly lovely, with every detail a sparkling jewel of enjoyment.

"It took him a while to get me to open up to him, but that resistance came from me. I could not believe my good luck and was waiting for fate to kick me in the teeth again."

Fate had turned friendly. Instead of disaster, Emily's romance with the manager prospered until one sunny day in June they were wed.

"No expense was spared, and the reception was written up in the papers," Emily said. "I enjoy all the creature comforts of the good life now, but above and beyond all that I've finally found the man who loves me and whom I can love in return.

"The *Eastern Air Technique* changed that old saying. For me it was fourth time lucky, not third!"

FIND TOTAL CONTENTMENT WITH SKYSCRAPER ATTRACTION

You will note as we proceed that several of the techniques of the Faces are almost identical. They differ only in the aims and symbols employed.

This is one such technique. You can see it as the East Face equivalent of the corresponding North Face technique. *Skyscraper Attraction* is very much like the *Amazing Triad Attunement* we discovered in Energy Circuit 3: only the Face, Symbols and desired end result are changed.

EAST FACE OF LOVE AND PEACE OF MIND

As before, view the *Blue Circle of Vayu* for a couple of minutes. Then pass your attention to the uppermost point of your *New Psychic Energy Generator.* Pretend you're standing atop the pyramid, with the Blue Circle sloping down the East Face below you.

Now, in your mind, bring up pictures of people you'd like to attract. "See" them standing in a group around the east base edge of your Generator. Have them crowd around with their heads thrown back, looking up at you at the apex. With that picture firmly in mind, pretend that the *Blue Circle of Vayu* is lighting up, sending blue light shining all over you. Mentally bask in this light and pretend the crowd down below is cheering and applauding you, as if you're the greatest rock and roll star in the business!

Hold that picture in your mind as firmly as you can for about 30 seconds. Then let it go, and terminate the exercise as usual. *Skyscraper Attraction* will do the rest!

TERRY V. WAS WRONG WHEN HE THOUGHT HE WAS TOO OLD FOR COMPLETE FULFILLMENT

"When you hit 70 you expect to have lost some of your old pizazz," Terry V. said. "But I was keenly disappointed to find my get-up-and-go had gotten-up-and-gone totally. I still nursed erotic ideas in my head, but that's where they had to stay; the rest of me just wouldn't raise a quiver to carry out my desires.

"Wrinkled face, thinning gray hair, dentures, failing eyes and arthritic joints were hardly likely to make me a favorite with the ladies. I guess if I'd had money I might have been able to get satisfaction—I read somewhere that although money does not buy love, it sure rents some fine affection!"

Terry had bought all manner of rejuvenation methods to try to recapture some of his natural energies, including herbs, vitamins, exercises and sundry mail order gadgets and potions.

96   *EAST FACE OF LOVE AND PEACE OF MIND*

"All useless," Terry reported. "Seemed like nothing was going to work for me. And even if I had gotten my aging body back into that kind of shape, I wondered who would be interested in an old goat like me."

During his continued search for the fountain of youth, Terry happened upon Pyramid Research. Like many others before him, he employed it as a last resort, anticipating as little success as he'd found with previous "miracle-working" methods.

"But I gave it my full shot," he said. "Never have been one for half measures, so I was prepared to give time and energy to it. *Skyscraper Attraction* was my key technique with some West Face additions."

The West Face methods are included in Energy Circuit 6 of this book. Terry's reading and practice of pyramid techniques made him something of an authority on the subject, and his friends took to calling him Terry the Pyramid Person.

"They laughed on the other sides of their faces when a lady reporter showed up from Florida," Terry said. "She'd picked up local gossip about me from another journalist and she thought there might be a story in my pyramid researches."

The resulting publicity brought Terry mail and calls from all over North America.

"For a short while I became the teacher of a group," he said. "I've gone on to greater things since. At the time it took me a while to realize *Skyscraper Attraction* was working as promised. I was indeed the center of an admiring group of people of all ages, with something they wanted. I'd become a minor celebrity!"

Among Terry's "pupils" was a trio of women who were skilled in many aspects of psychism and the occult, but who had never mastered Pyramid Energy techniques.

"That became a two-way street," Terry said. "I instructed them in Pyramid Energy, and in exchange they gave me a course in a most fascinating subject: Sex Magic."

EAST FACE OF LOVE AND PEACE OF MIND

Terry is not prepared to reveal the secrets of that latter subject, although he says he might write a book about it one day.

"Final results of my involvement with pyramids is that I'm duly admired for my knowledge. But much more than that, I've regained my natural energies," Terry said. "You can forget about my previous physical failings—they're in the past.

"I thought I was too old for complete fulfillment, but I'm pleased to report that tuning in to Pyramid Energy has proven me mistaken!"

ENSLAVE YOUR LOVE TARGET WITH THE MULTIPLE QUADRATIC ENCIRCLEMENT

At the outset I must tell you that this is not my favorite East Face technique. Its overtones of domination are out of line with my personal psychology, and (given the choice) I prefer to see people attract and manipulate by example rather than forcibly shape their fellow beings.

However, several people known to me have found a need to use this technique and have employed it (they say) with great success. So, for the sake of offering as many tools as possible to you, after much thought I have included it.

But personally I suggest you use all other love and peace techniques before this one, employing the *Multiple Quadratic Encirclement* only as a last resort.

This technique requires that you know *whom* you wish to enslave, and you should be able to call up a clear mind picture of him or her when required.

View the *Blue Circle of Vayu* in the usual manner, then turn your eyes to the apex point. Imagine yourself to be standing 'way up there, looking down into the interior of the Generator, through a skylight which you also should envisage.

98   EAST FACE OF LOVE AND PEACE OF MIND

In the space below, pretend your love target is imprisoned, enclosed by the four sloping walls of your Generator.

Mentally turn and look down at the south-east, south-west, north-west and north-east corners of your Generator, in that order. This means, in your mind, you make a full turn to the right. Then transfer your attention back to the *Blue Circle of Vayu*, looking at it as you allow the mental tableau to dissolve. Spend a few seconds on regarding the Blue Circle before concluding the experiment.

Placing this mental playlet in the Unseen on a regular basis puts the desired result of love enslavement of the party concerned firmly into your future.

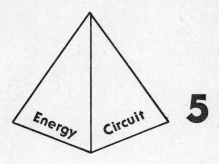

The South Face of Protection and Offense

In this powerful section you will find I have inserted my own beliefs and philosophies—possibly they're biases—when advising when and how to use these powers we're investigating.

The South Face is undeniably one of the most titanic sources of energy when you tune in to it, and that energy, connected with Fire, can be used equally for good or evil.

We're all too familiar with the evil aspects of Fire: arson, murder and war are but three examples of symbolic Fire being used to cause loss and hurt.

I'm well aware that few of my readers will wish to use South Face attunement for evil purposes. Even if they try, it will not operate for them if their sole motive is to cause pain and harm.

Yet when we actually examine motives behind actions, we can sometimes see suffering being caused even though the underlying motive intends no such negativity. And motive, the ultimate aim, is the driving force behind all psychic energy techniques, and when we're using symbolic Fire, the results

100 SOUTH FACE OF PROTECTION AND OFFENSE

can indeed be harmful to others. Whether they seem to deserve harm or not, I feel personally that inflicting pain on others to be undesirable, no matter what the justification.

The Vietnam War is a classic example of symbolic Fire causing massive chaos and hurt, even though the guiding *motives* were good: no one could call aiding an oppressed people a *bad* motive, yet we can see the turmoil which resulted from such squeaky-clean motives.

The simple point I'm trying to impress on you is that when you use Fire for attack or offense, you need to be careful what the end results are. *New Psychic Energy Power* will prevent anything ultimately bad from happening to you, but in my reckoning it's probably better not to place yourself potentially in the position of collecting negativity from others by hurting them.

So my invariable suggestion when I am asked to commit myself is that *protection* techniques generally bring happier results overall than *offense* techniques.

On the other hand it would be foolish of me to pretend that such offensive techniques do not exist. Offense and attack have their uses, and I would be the last person to deny that. You can, in fact, see where they've been used with excellent effects by subjects in the case histories here. All I suggest, then, is that you try protection routines *first,* using the more energetic attack techniques as final measures if the protection routines do not solve your problems.

ATTACK AND OFFENSE DECISIONS ARE SIMPLE WITH NEW PSYCHIC POWER ENERGY

As already stated, *New Psychic Energy Power* will not permit you to hurt someone who does not deserve it. What it *will* do is return in equal measure any negativity that is directed at you.

So when deciding which *South Face* method best suits your purpose, all you need to do is ask yourself a few simple

SOUTH FACE OF PROTECTION AND OFFENSE 101

questions about the subject you intend to work upon. Your
honest answers to these questions will assuredly direct you to
the correct Fire technique to employ.

• "Has this person, group or situation caused me actual
physical harm?" If so, you can use the devastating *Southern
Fire Technique* to cause your tormenter equal material loss or
pain. But if your target has not assaulted you or touched you
or your material assets, the *Southern Fire Technique* will not
be effective.

• "Has this person, group or situation caused me *mental*
turmoil or pain?" If the answer to that question is in the
affirmative, the *Scarlet Triangle of Tejas* is your weapon to
employ most effectively. However, if you merely fear or believe
you're going to be hurt, the Scarlet Triangle is not being used
at its full potential.

• "Is this person, group or situation blocking me from
progress without actually causing me harm?" That kind of
situation calls for the *Mystic Pentafork Method* which swiftly
turns opposition into cooperation.

• "Is this person, group or situation one which may be
opposing me, even though I have only circumstantial evidence to suggest this?" Here we find a situation where your
hunches suggest you're being held back, even if you have no
solid proof that would stand up in a court of law. So use the
Sunshine Protection Routine. If you are indeed being
obstructed, the obstacles will vanish. If you happen to be
wrong in your estimation of the situation, no harm will be
done.

• "Is this person, group or situation opposing me personally, without necessarily being negative toward me?" This
could describe the situation when City Hall passes a by-law
which adversely affects the quality of your life, yet has not
been especially aimed at you. It may, in fact, have been
created with the best of intentions, so that its perpetrators
would be amazed to find someone is being inconvenienced

102 SOUTH FACE OF PROTECTION AND OFFENSE

and upset by it. This is the type of circumstance which the *Sympathetic Portrayal Technique* can quickly put to rights, enabling you to once again live your life to the full.

PAT Q. MYSTERIOUSLY VANQUISHED HER ENEMIES

"When you're going it alone in this cruel world you need to be stronger than your fellow beings," avers Pat Q. "Insecure people who need the protection of a group or the paternal guardianship of an employer seem to focus in on you as if you are a revolutionary who should be executed.

"I'm not much for being protected from cradle to grave by any government in exchange for doing as I'm told by a boss. I'm one of the free spirits of this world, carving my own path, taking my bruises as they come and not running whining to welfare agencies when the going gets tough. If I'm in trouble, that's my fault and I'll battle my own way out."

Pat is a free-lance artist and, as you may have gathered, is very forthright in her opinions on freedom. In a checkered career she has seen both feasting and fasting, but says she has done more of the former since she discovered Pyramid Energy.

"The prime way to get ahead is to overcome the opposition," she said. "If I'm ever harassed or obstructed I use a South Face technique. Most often it's the *Mystic Pentafork Method* that turns things around for me."

Pat's most memorable use of that method occurred a couple of years before she soared to the forefront of the art world. At the time she was a gifted but struggling unknown in New York.

"I saw myself as being in competition with the rest of the art community," she said, "but in particular a local group in the Village was stopping my progress. I could not say they

SOUTH FACE OF PROTECTION AND OFFENSE 103

were causing me physical obstruction, but their sneaky ways were making sure I had to fight every inch of the way."

Typical of the low tactics her opponents used was their making sure that Pat could never find space to exhibit her paintings in local studios.

"They spread half-truths about me and my work," she said, "suggesting I was unreliable and might not provide paintings to fill allocated spaces. They also implied my works had no artistic merit and would downgrade the reputation of the gallery if they were shown.

"False telephone calls from alleged clients found me running across town to non-existent addresses at the precise time an art critic was in the vicinity of my home. If I'd been able to show the critic some of my work, as later happened, I'd have gained acceptance and sales much quicker."

Adept at many intuitive disciplines, Pat mastered Pyramid Energy in a short time.

"As a student of form and harmony I could see the logic of aligning with Tides of energy," she said, "and as I work with symbolism a great deal, the Elemental symbols on my *New Psychic Energy Generator* had great meaning for me.

"I especially found wisdom and truth within the five-armed Fire symbol, and the *Mystic Pentafork Method* had a certain mental majesty and force I knew would do my bidding."

She was right. Only days later some of her tormenters went to jail on drug-related charges. Others turned their attention to other unfortunates, while the rest simply dropped out of sight.

Pat soon found her rightful level in the world of art. Today you can see her work in gracious homes throughout the world, and sitters pay thousands of dollars to come to her penthouse studio to have her paint their portraits.

"How it worked I do not know," she said, "but I'm convinced of the authenticity of Pyramid Energy. I'm flowing neatly with all the Tides, and any enemies I may still have are unable to touch me. They're all vanquished for good."

104 SOUTH FACE OF PROTECTION AND OFFENSE

NOTHING BAD CAN TOUCH YOU WHEN YOU
USE THE SCARLET TRIANGLE OF TEJAS

Just as you have previously created the Yellow Square and the Blue Circle, now you need to make a bright red (scarlet) triangle to place against the South Face of your *New Psychic Energy Generator.*

As before, a paper symbol is all you require, and a simple way to make the three-sided piece you need is to cut the corner off a piece of paper with one straight cut. Another way of creating a triangle is to draw a capital letter "A" and cut around its outline, erasing the horizontal crossbar afterward.

Having already made two other symbols and placed them against their respective faces, I need to offer little explanation to you on securing the Scarlet Triangle against the South Face of your *New Psychic Energy Generator.* The South Face is the one the sun shines on fully at noon, if your Generator sits on a window sill ... provided you live north of the equator.

You've now placed a strong protective symbol which can attune you with the South Face Tide which protects, defends and (where needed) attacks.

Remember what we're doing in these exercises. If you're under attack, repressed, blocked or hassled, at basic metaphysical levels this means you've somehow gotten yourself out of the main stream of the South Tide. Contemplation of the *Scarlet Triangle of Tejas* will change that for you in short order.

Set up the usual conditions and look at the Scarlet Triangle steadily for about two minutes, then allow your eyes to close gently. Just as when you viewed the Blue Circle, there are no demands on you to do more than sit quietly now. However, if your brain insists on fussing about things which seem important, think about less pressing matters as advised for the Blue Circle exercise.

This apparently insignificant routine can have tremen-

SOUTH FACE OF PROTECTION AND OFFENSE 105

dously large results. Any specific situation or person immediately begins to lose the ability to cause you mental turmoil.

Keep your eyes closed for another two minutes or so, open them to view the Triangle for another 30 seconds, then continue with your regular chores.

A few minutes spent on contemplating the Scarlet Triangle on any day you can manage it will work miracles of detachment and peace for you.

"IT'S BETTER THAN HAVING A GUARDIAN ANGEL," ATTESTS REGINALD Y.

Reginald Y. is a firm supporter of the *Scarlet Triangle of Tejas.* His problem is not unusual: his mother-in-law was causing him much mental anguish.

"Very subtle she was," Reginald said. "No way was she doing anything to me I could call material or physical damage. She did things which kept me on edge, chipping away at the stability of our marriage."

For example, Reginald would become furious when his mother-in-law dropped by when the big game was on TV and insisted he turn it off because she had some important matter to discuss which could not wait.

"After she'd talked for three hours and the game was over I would realize she was just wasting my time," Reginald said. "Her 'important matter' would be nothing more critical than the relative merits of cornflakes or oats for breakfast or some similar triviality."

Worse was the innuendo his mother-in-law would insert into discussions about Reginald with his wife.

"She would ask all sorts of questions with an air of total innocence," Reginald said. "Such as 'How can you be sure your husband is playing poker with his *male* friends on Saturdays?' Or she'd drop odd remarks into the conversation about cheating husbands and how many were known to be having affairs with their secretaries.

106   *SOUTH FACE OF PROTECTION AND OFFENSE*

"Another sweet little number was to offer to help with the car installments as if I'd run us into debt and was about to be hauled off to jail for non-payment. Or she'd bring some delicacy and hand it to my wife, saying. 'I'm sure this is something you cannot afford on the money your husband gives you.'

"She always called me 'your husband' and made it sound as if I was a dirty old lecher who was keeping her daughter imprisoned in sin."

Reginald's wife was intimidated by her mother and would never strike back, and the strain in the air after the old lady had left was almost visible to the unaided eye.

"It got so I dreaded seeing her car pull into the driveway," Reginald related. "I would worry in advance about what new torture she had devised.

"One thing I'll say for her, she was consistent. Always put me down whenever we met, and it only confirmed her stated opinion that I was 'an immature loser' when I occasionally blew my cork at her. But she had a skin like a rhino and always came back with more of her mischief."

A clear case for Pyramid Energy to come to the rescue. How Reginald came across the *Scarlet Triangle of Tejas* perhaps confirms one of his mother-in-law's suspicious remarks.

"Things were so stressful I was indeed looking at my secretary as a chance to cheat," Reginald admitted. "But that passionate affair got no further than a coffee and sandwich one time only at a fastfood restaurant after work. A very perceptive girl, is my secretary. She'd already recognized the symptoms and was not about to spoil a good job by having an affair with her boss.

"Over coffee she got me talking. I was scornful when she told me of the miracles Pyramid Energy could work. But right there at the table she had me build a little pyramid from a blank file card from my briefcase. The waitress thought we were crazy as I sketched on the symbols and stuck bits of colored paper on the four sides."

SOUTH FACE OF PROTECTION AND OFFENSE   107

In the crowded cafe Reginald was instructed in how to view the Scarlet Triangle.

"Exactly the right phrase is to say it worked like a charm," Reginald said. "When I arrived home my heart sank to see my mother-in-law's car in front of the house. There I was, a full hour late, and I knew exactly how much mileage she'd make of that."

Reginald walked into his home to meet a verbal creeping barrage. His mother-in-law was in top form.

"She made me sound like a wife-beater, child molester, drug smuggler, indecent exposer, deserter and dedicated drunk," Reginald said. "Previously I'd have reacted and snarled at her. This time I smiled like the Mona Lisa and listened until she ran out of steam.

"Finally she stopped and there was silence for minutes. I was totally relaxed, smoking and sipping a coffee while waiting for my wife to serve supper. My mother-in-law actually spluttered in confusion and annoyance when I refused to be goaded into anger.

"She tried several more ploys during the meal but it all went straight over my head. From that day to this she's never been able to ruffle my feathers even a trifle. I got to be sorry for the neurotic old biddy when I realized she was lonely, and jealous because I'd 'stolen' her daughter from her."

Eventually his mother-in-law grew tired of her fruitless harassment, seeing it now no longer had the intended effect of annoying Reginald.

"What a difference," Reginald said. "She's almost human now. And to think it all began the night I met the *Scarlet Triangle of Tejas*. Amazing!"

OVERCOMING OPPOSITION WITH THE SYMPATHETIC PORTRAYAL TECHNIQUE

Whose cooperation do you need? Maybe you require a loan from a stiff-necked credit manager. Perhaps your boss is

108 *SOUTH FACE OF PROTECTION AND OFFENSE*

resisting giving you a raise you deserve. Your companion may be refusing to assist you in some vital project. Somewhere along the line of life we inevitably run into opposition of a type which needs only a sharp nudge at esoteric levels to bring a change of heart and smiling agreement.

Try the *Sympathetic Portrayal Technique* at such times. You'll be amazed at the results: you perform a simple mental routine, and the consequences appear quickly (sometimes instantly) in the material world.

You should apply the *Sympathetic Portrayal Technique* at the precise time when you fear you're going to get a refusal from someone.

Let's use that credit manager as an example. When you meet, recall a mental picture of the Scarlet Triangle, and pretend you are looking *through* the triangle at the person you're being interviewed by.

As you talk, discuss or make your case, continue to pretend to yourself that you're talking through the triangle. See it as a transparent red filter which allows your words and ideas to go through, like coffee going through a drip filter paper.

That's the only thing you need to do. If you've been working regularly at contemplating the *Scarlet Triangle of Tejas,* your batting average for getting cooperation from previously obdurate opponents will increase sharply and amazingly.

JEAN W. SECURED A COVETED WELL-PAID POSITION

High unemployment and lack of personal qualifications were hitting hard at Jean W. For months she had been tramping the cold wet streets of Chicago looking for work.

"My shoes were so thin I could have stood on a dime and told you if it was head or tail," she said. "But at that time, if I'd had a dime, I'd have put it toward a bite to eat."

SOUTH FACE OF PROTECTION AND OFFENSE

The dollar may have been depressed but Jean refused to be the same.

"I had little going for me. Not much learning, a lot of odd jobs in my time with nothing long-lasting or secure, a spell in a remand home years back when I was a wild kid—all strikes against me," she related. "About my only plus was I'm bright and willing, given a chance."

That chance eluded her. Each day she woke shivering in her squalid little room, cold with the chill of not enough food and stiff with unrested, aching limbs. Her funds were almost exhausted and her final unemployment check had arrived the previous week.

"More days of knocking on doors and making calls had given me nothing more than 'We'll let you know' or "Sorry, the vacancy has been filled.' I started panhandling for quarters as I walked wearily from block to block," she said. "I'd sunk that low, but I got little joy, and when the weeping gray sky turned dark I headed for my room. It was drier than the streets if I kept the newspaper stuffed in the broken window, and I had companionship—the roaches who seemed as hungry as I was."

Slumped hopelessly on her sagging cot, Jean was startled when someone knocked gently on her door. Only one person came calling and that was the rent collector. She knew his knock only too well; as her rent slipped further behind, his peremptory thump on her door grew heavier.

"I called out, asking who it was, and a guy outside said he lived across the hall and could he see me a minute," Jean said. "I'd seen him going in and out. Beard, jeans and beads—not your average mugger or rapist—so I opened the door."

An hour later Jean was feeling a combination of optimism and skepticism.

"The guy said he'd overheard me using the phone in the hallway and knew I needed a job," she said. "He had news of a vacancy I might be able to fill. But the extra curve he threw at me was to show me a little pyramid and explain what he

110 SOUTH FACE OF PROTECTION AND OFFENSE

called *New Psychic Energy Power* methods. He briefed me in making a pyramid for myself and how to carry out a little routine called the *Sympathetic Portrayal Technique.*

"Seemed to be a bunch of pure baloney to me, but I had nothing else to do in the long hours before sleep came so I did as he said and built a little pyramid with all its trimmings."

Next day Jean went to the address she'd been given and ran into a large obstacle.

"The interviewing guy was a creep," she said. "He made it clear he was against me from the start. I'm no Miss America, and shortage of cash had made sure I'd win no fashion contests. But added to that the interviewer coldly told me they had no need for any more black people on the staff ... only he did not call me black: he used a real insulting Southern word.

"But that did not stop him from making a pass at me right there in the office, and he was visibly angry when I told him what he could do."

Yet Jean really needed the job, and in it she would be working for that prejudiced man. The vacancy was precisely fitted to being handled by Jean, but somehow she had to get by this obstructive male.

"I remembered the *Sympathetic Portrayal Technique,*" she said, "and called to mind the Scarlet Triangle as my friend had suggested.

"From that moment on the interviewer began to thaw. He stopped looking down my blouse, interrupted himself as he was listing the reasons why I would not fit into the organization, and began listing my advantages instead.

"He sent out for coffee and cookies, and about 30 minutes later he smiled and asked when I could start work."

Jean says she's not the richest person in Chicago now but she's working steadily at a job she enjoys. She is gradually getting her life into shape, and has a more opulent apartment with heat and comforts.

"Having seen that Pyramid Energy turned a sour and opposing man into the soul of cooperation, I'm convinced it

SOUTH FACE OF PROTECTION AND OFFENSE 111

works," she said. "I only wish I could run into that bearded dude again to learn some more techniques from him."

DISPEL NEGATIVE OR EVIL CONDITIONS
WITH THE SOUTHERN FIRE TECHNIQUE

As I pointed out earlier in this Energy Circuit, the *Southern Fire Technique* is remarkably powerful, but it does have specialized applications.

Up front, you can use it with success on an "eye for an eye, tooth for a tooth" basis. However, should you find that Biblical thought conflicting with your belief that you should "turn the other cheek" (another concept from the same Book), you'd better think awhile before you set out to use this technique. If smashing your enemy is going to make you feel guilty and worried, the cure could be worse than the existing disease!

And to repeat the basic necessity for this method: use it *only* on people who have caused you actual *material or physical* harm.

That word "physical" is important. In order to cause material hurt, the perpetrator has used energy, probably muscular energy. You are going to locate that energy at esoteric levels and return it whence it came, backed by similar motives of negativity with which it was applied to you.

Put yourself in your regular position for viewing your *New Psychic Energy Generator,* with the *Scarlet Triangle of Tejas* clearly in your line of sight. Look at it for about two minutes, then close your eyes.

Now fish around in your memory and bring up a clear replay of the event or events which caused you the pain or harm which you wish to repel.

> *NOTE: If at this stage you find it a problem bringing back clear and precise memories of the event and the parties concerned, this could be a sign that the situation is less critical than you believe. If you're having trouble recalling*

112 SOUTH FACE OF PROTECTION AND OFFENSE

it clearly, it's probably not bugging you as much as you believe it to be. In such a case, stop this routine before going any further.

This memory work "calls back" the energy used in the event, and you should now feel yourself getting warm, cold, hot, or maybe moderately agitated. *If there is no change in the way you feel,* interrupt the routine and do something else: you're receiving clear evidence that the situation is less important than you feel it to be, and is not worth wasting effort on.

As you experience this energy phenomenon, imagine the energy you've generated flowing away from you and entering the *Scarlet Triangle of Tejas.*

That has put the wheels in motion, and destiny will take care of the affair from here on in. Open your eyes, look at the Scarlet Triangle for a few seconds, then go about your business.

FLOYD J. REPELLED A BLACK MAGIC ATTACK

"I was hurt, bewildered and ready to die," Floyd J. records. "How I got into that mess is ancient history now. My case is a warning to people who choose to dabble in witchcraft and the black arts.

"About a year before I reached the hairy edge of screaming madness and terror I had joined a society in Louisiana after answering an ad that promised to reveal to me secrets of voodoo and magic."

Floyd duly met the leader of the society and paid a heavy initiation fee.

"I was doomed to pay far more as the months passed," Floyd said. "Yet the money was not the chief factor. I was also paying in loss of self-respect, in being dominated by a powerful occultist and in seeing my life crumbling into ruins."

SOUTH FACE OF PROTECTION AND OFFENSE 113

Floyd will not talk about the degrading rituals he was involved with, nor the terrifying sacrifices and ceremonies he took part in.

"The black magic was working," he said. "I was indeed getting my desires for power and wealth. But most of the money went to the society and I was becoming mentally disturbed. Sleep came late, my health suffered and my nerves were shot.

"Before I lost my reason entirely I told the High Priest I was cutting loose and going my own way. I was horrified when he grinned like Satan and said I could not do that—the blood ceremonies I'd taken part in made me his disciple for life. If I quit, he would pursue me with curses and evil."

Floyd nevertheless fled and vowed never to go near the Black Temple again.

"The society followed me and made my life hell on earth," he recalls. "They used their black powers to weaken my will, to disorganize my bodily functions, to turn people against me and to transform me into a frightened sleepless wreck. I could not believe the hollow-eyed skeletal face I saw when I looked in a mirror was truly me.

"They added physical assault to their spells. Evil-smelling liquids were poured under my front door. They slashed the tires of my car. The High Priest would call me in the dark hours before dawn and whisper obscene threats. Then a thug beat me up on the street, and told me the Black Chief would stop all this if I'd return to their Temple."

Floyd resorted to his own defenses. He worked all the psychic self-defense rituals he had learned during his occult studies.

"None of them was effective," he said. "Strange vapors began coiling through my room after midnight. Invisible slimy things left trails like giant slugs across my bed. Scratching on my doors began—and nothing visible was there.

"I was on the brink of madness when Pyramid Energy came to my aid."

114   *SOUTH FACE OF PROTECTION AND OFFENSE*

Floyd had appealed to another powerful occultist to help him.

"That man told me he could do little for me himself, but he could show me how to help myself," Floyd said. "He told me about the *Southern Fire Technique*, saying it was one of the most protective techniques he could give me, and fitted to my desperate circumstances.

"At the time I figured it was no more potent than the other methods I'd tried and seen fail miserably."

Yet Floyd was free of the evil influences within one week.

"The first working of the *Southern Fire Technique* saw the departure of the horrible phenomena in and around my home," he said. "Next day I was called as a witness for the prosecution who needed to prove a man had committed second degree murder. He turned out to be the thug who had beaten me, and my evidence of his viciousness helped to put him away for ten years.

"The Black Temple was the scene of a spectacular unexplained fire that week. It burned clear down to the basement, destroying it utterly. The High Priest was burned as he rushed into the fire to retrieve some of his Black Grimoires and icons. He is scarred for life, almost blind, walks with a cane and has lost the use of one hand.

"His acolytes all suffered varying degrees of injury or misfortune, apparently by accident."

Floyd has had no further trouble from the society, but he has made a solemn vow never to meddle in the black arts again.

"Who needs them?" he says. "I've now got something infinitely more powerful and truly holy. Pyramid Energy is my path from here on in."

DEFEATING YOUR ENEMIES WITH THE SUNSHINE PROTECTION ROUTINE

This fascinating technique is extremely useful when you're having trouble putting your finger on the precise cause

SOUTH FACE OF PROTECTION AND OFFENSE 115

of your problems. You suspect someone or something is standing in the way of your progress, but have no real evidence to prove it.

So use the *Sunshine Protection Routine,* another powerful method of attuning yourself with the South Face Tide and batting away any obstructions to your planned path to peace, prosperity and plenitude.

Begin viewing the *Scarlet Triangle of Tejas* under your usual conditions. Look at it for the regular two minutes or so, then close your eyes. Push away fears and worries by thinking about peaceful surroundings, as in preceding techniques, but add one extra feature to your mind pictures.

Recall how the sun looks when it shines on calm water on a bright sunny day; think about the deep shadows which the sun casts from trees and buildings. Then recall your *own* shadow as it would lie on the ground if the sun were shining on you at this moment. Then pretend you're turning to *face* the sun, and you feel its warmth on your face, and your shadow falls behind you.

If you can carry out this routine when the sun actually shines on your face, arrange it that way. *But do not open your eyes to look at the sun.* That can be ultimately dangerous to your eyesight. Staring at the sun can be a quick and direct path to total blindness.

After bathing your face in the real or imagined sunlight for about a minute, turn your face to your *New Psychic Energy Generator,* open your eyes and view the Scarlet Triangle for another half-minute before concluding the routine.

JUDY I. SAYS, "ALL MY OBSTRUCTIONS FADED AWAY LIKE MAGIC"

"Why can I not get ahead? Will my troubles last for the rest of my miserable life? Was I born under an evil star? Does someone hate me? Where am I going wrong?"

116   *SOUTH FACE OF PROTECTION AND OFFENSE*

Such questions occur to many of us at stages in our lives, and Judy I. had reached just such an impasse.

"I used to wake with a dull, heavy feeling, dreading what the day would bring. Nothing I did was right," she said. "No way could I put a finger on who or what was holding me back, but I failed at every turn."

Apart from hundreds of petty irritations, Judy found the quality of her life being eroded by unhappy events. She saw less worthy people at work promoted over her head. Her application for a better apartment in her block was mislaid and another party secured the prime location Judy had been coveting for months. Her paycheck was misprinted by a computer and the bank refused to cash it.

Her car unaccountably developed an expensive malady in its electric system and three tires punctured inside 14 days. Her TV broke down, a dryer at the laundromat scorched an expensive pantsuit, and her shower blocked, overflowed and ruined a hall rug she had just laid down.

Her boyfriend walked out after a misunderstanding and relocated two states away.

"It was ridiculous. If something could go wrong, it did," Judy said. "Nothing truly catastrophic, but the cumulative effect was wearing me to a frazzle. I seemed to have run into a combination of opposition from people and blows from an uncaring fate.

"I began to wonder when it would end, if ever. Worse: I began to worry that it would get steadily worse and I'd end up destitute and diseased."

Airing her misfortunes to a friend, Judy was introduced to Pyramid Energy.

"The result of a long and interesting discussion about pyramid research was that I decided to see if the *Scarlet Triangle of Tejas* could help me," Judy said. "From what my friend told me, it seemed the *Sunshine Protection Routine* could put me on a path back to serenity."

Pyramid Energy duly came up trumps for Judy. Her regular practice with the Scarlet Triangle coincided with quick improvement in her life style and conditions.

SOUTH FACE OF PROTECTION AND OFFENSE   117

"The list would be endless if I wrote down all the happy things that came my way," Judy said. "Bottom line was where I'd been doing everything wrong, I now hit a delightful phase of being in the right place at the right time—and that's continued ever since.

"I zapped to administrative levels at work, leapfrogging above those people who'd passed me in earlier promotions. I met a car salesman at a disco, he traded my old banger for a new Monza, we fell in love and married.

Some of Judy's good luck rubbed off on her new husband. He was made area representative for a major vehicle distributor and he and Judy were soon on easy street.

"I keep my *New Psychic Energy Generator* in the window with the ocean view," Judy said, "so when we sit down for cocktails before dining in our solarium we can absorb some more of the Pyramid Energy tuning-in benefits.

"Now all my obstructive influences have faded away like magic, and I know what enjoying life is all about."

BAD IS SWIFTLY TRANSFORMED INTO GOOD WHEN YOU EMPLOY THE MYSTIC PENTAFORK METHOD

After reading the above headline, your first question may well be, "What's a Mystic Pentafork?" Simple answer: it's the name of the Fire Symbol you inscribed on the South Face of your *New Psychic Energy Generator.*

Attaching its powers to your destiny path with the following method can work miracles of change, with previous opposers quickly becoming cooperative and supportive.

Make a small diagram of the Mystic Pentafork on a piece of paper, just as you did for the Air Symbol for the *Eastern Air Technique* in Energy Circuit 4.

Sit yourself down in your now familiar position, and view the *Scarlet Triangle of Tejas* for two minutes. Then transfer your attention to the Pentafork which you can be holding or have placed suitably in front of you.

118 SOUTH FACE OF PROTECTION AND OFFENSE

After a few seconds of gazing at the Pentafork, close your eyes. Consider why you're performing this routine, and what results you wish to be forthcoming. Think seriously about those results, and pretend that what you wish to occur has already happened.

Open your eyes, view the Mystic Pentafork for about ten seconds, return your gaze to the Scarlet Triangle for a further 30 seconds, then terminate this routine.

Put your Mystic Pentafork in your purse or wallet, and carry it with you, as you did with the Air Symbol. Of course, when you carry out this *Mystic Pentafork Method* again (and you should schedule it on a regular basis for best effects), you can use the same symbol for viewing; no need to draw a new one each time.

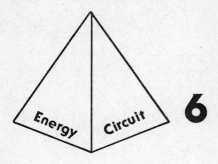

The West Face of Health and Strength

I place good health second only to peace of mind in the list of attributes needed to attain supreme happiness and fulfillment. Without a healthy body, many of life's pleasures are flawed. So I heartily recommend regular application of these West Face routines, to put yourself in harmony with the glories of the West Face Tide which can help to sweep away physical pains, dispel disease and enable your body to heal whatever is ailing you.

PYRAMID ENERGY CIRCUITS AND YOUR DOCTOR: AN UNBEATABLE TEAM!

Please read, absorb and inwardly digest the following vital point: *Under no circumstances must you attempt to use West Face routines to replace qualified medical care.*

You'll find me one of the first to applaud the efforts of psychic and spiritual healers, and to witness the miracles they have performed, sometimes in apparently hopeless cases. They are channels for West Face-type energies, and can bring to a sick person metaphysical vibrations which, by some as yet undefined means, bring healing to bodily malfunctions.

Yet I award an equal amount of applause to the dedicated efforts of those we may call orthodox healers of medical science.

Despite occasional adverse publicity for the few, most doctors know what they are doing and have an impressive battery of healing aids at their fingertips. Properly applied, surgery, drugs and medical therapy are *the* answers to curing disease.

I feel that people are foolish who try to ignore or denigrate the incredible strides medical science has taken in its painstaking research across the centuries. But similarly, I feel that spiritual healing and psychic methods deserve to be researched more sympathetically and thoroughly than they have been to date. Some alleged "healers" are indeed heartless charlatans, but other healers who use psychic methods have too good a track record to be ignored and dismissed.

So I suggest you give psychic powers and science equal chances to heal anything that is wrong with you. If you need medical treatment, see your doctor: but *add* the West Face energies to help things along.

Generally speaking I would advise you *not* to tell your doctor you're assisting him by calling on metaphysical energies. We still have far to go before the medical fraternity as a whole is prepared to accept such precepts.

If you have a minor sickness which you'd ordinarily treat yourself by visiting your local pharmacy, add the West Face techniques to your pill or potion: you'll get better quicker. In fact I can say with all due caution that if you're going to take a *non-prescription* drug to clear your discomfort, you could try an initial dose of West Face Tide techniques before you buy the medication. You may just find that you've saved yourself a few dollars!

WEST FACE OF HEALTH AND STRENGTH 121

And if you have a chronic condition which the specialists have told you they can do nothing more to alleviate or cure, by all means move in with West Face energies. You could amaze the experts by getting well—although again it might be best to give credit to modern science rather than insist you did it yourself by tuning in to invisible energy tides. If you're no longer sick, does it *really* matter how or why you got well?

My recommendation is that you use West Face techniques *in conjunction with* any medical diagnoses, prescriptions and directions, and thus you'll get the best of both worlds.

CHARLIE G. IS FIT AFTER BEING GIVEN SIX MONTHS TO LIVE

If you re-read the introduction to James I.'s case history at the beginning of this book you will recognize the similarity in my style of presentation. I make no claims that Pyramid Energy ever *cured* anyone: under the right conditions, be they medical, mental, psychic or any combination of the three, the body heals itself.

Charlie G., 72, is a retired crane-driver. At age 65, after having stubbornly resisted unusual and recurring spells of exhaustion for years, Charlie consulted his physician. Blood tests revealed chronic leukemia in an advanced state. The most optimistic forecast was progressive deterioration resulting in death within six months.

The doctor told Charlie his diagnosis, and regular treatment was begun.

Charlie, a resilient and fatalistic man, put his affairs in order. But he was "not about to lie down and turn belly up for any bunch of cancer cells" if he could avoid it.

As one of his supplementary treatments, Charlie went to the Philippines to undergo treatment by psychic surgeons. He reports that various psychic "operations" were carried out,

122   WEST FACE OF HEALTH AND STRENGTH

allegedly removing tumors from his ear, stomach and chest. His doctors had previously detected no tumors by X-ray and other diagnostic techniques.

The leukemia progressed as anticipated. Charlie took to a diet of grapes, an alleged cancer alleviator in some unconfirmed cases. He also investigated and took several herbal products, including one from a Mexican clinic.

"The cancer specialists were interested in my attempts to stop the leukemia, so long as I continued with their orthodox therapy," Charlie said. "I was quite surprised at their open-minded approach. One doctor told me if I could be cured he did not care if it was done with burnt feathers and animal entrails: his job was to do his best to heal me the best way he knew how and so long as I did nothing to negate his attempts he would not complain.

"He admitted some evidence exists which seems to suggest cancer undergoes remission for some patients when they apply additional mental therapy. So he was interested, but non-committal, when I told him I had been using the *Six-Rayed Star Thought* as an application of Pyramid Energy."

Charlie's deadline with death came and passed. He remained alive, and his leukemia was pronounced stable, but not cured. Seven years after the original diagnosis Charlie is active and fit. Latest medical reports cautiously suggest his leukemia has undergone remission and his life is no longer in danger.

HEALTH BLOSSOMS WHEN YOU APPLY THE SILVER CRESCENT OF APAS

A small piece of ordinary aluminum foil such as housewives use to wrap sandwiches plays an integral part in this West Face Energy Circuit. You need to create a crescent from the foil, the shape of a new moon, but somewhat fatter, about half an inch in size.

Find a round spice bottle or pill container about 1¼ to 1½ inches in diameter, or anything else circular of that size

WEST FACE OF HEALTH AND STRENGTH

that you can draw around. Stand your pattern on a piece of paper and draw a circle around its base, using the edge of the pattern to guide your pencil.

Now move the pattern about half an inch to one side and draw another circle around it. The resulting two intersecting circles will make a crescent shape. Two, in fact, although you need only one of them. Figure 4 shows the kind of double circle you should have drawn. Cut out one crescent (shown as the bolder line on the figure), and use that as a pattern to cut the same shape from a sheet of aluminum foil.

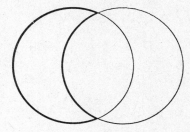

FIGURE 4: Pattern for Silver Crescent of Apas

This crescent of aluminum is your physical representation of your *Silver Crescent of Apas*. Secure it against the West Face of your *New Psychic Energy Generator*. That's the face the setting sun would shine on, the face opposite the East Face.

The Silver Crescent, your *New Psychic Energy Generator* and you form an Energy Circuit which can tune your body in harmony with the healing West Face Tide, and as a result blooming health surges through you.

"I'VE HAD NO REPEAT OF MY ARTHRITIS PAINS," AVOWS 83-YEAR-OLD EILEEN U.

The following is extracted from a letter received by one of my colleagues who is researching Pyramid Energy.

WEST FACE OF HEALTH AND STRENGTH

Arthritis first began in my hands at the age of 69. Later my hips were affected. Painkilling drugs enabled me to get about but the condition worsened as the years passed. By my late 70's I was a virtual cripple.

I visited as many specialists as my medical insurance would cover, and gained some relief, but nothing resembling a cure.

During my clinical treatment I joined with a spiritual search circle meeting at a Spiritualist Church near my home. A visiting lecturer spoke on Pyramid Power and extolled the virtues of West Face Tide methods in general and the Silver Crescent of Apas in particular.

I sat regularly with the circle, gazing on the Silver Crescent as we had been advised. On my 80th birthday, about a year after being introduced to the Silver Crescent, my doctor gave me a new pain-killer he said would be effective and non-addictive. I should take the tablets whenever the pains were at their worst.

I took the pills as prescribed and the pains receded from the first dose. To my surprise they never came back and I have had only one repeat of my pains in the intervening three years.

During a two-week vacation I missed my regular Silver Crescent exercises, and by the time I returned home I was feeling shooting pains in my joints which came some eight hours after using the prescribed medication.

Resuming my Silver Crescent work, I have had no repeat of my arthritis pains. (—Eileen U., Maine.)

REGAIN BLOOMING YOUTH WITH THE REVERSE TIME TABLEAU

When you're using any of the West Face techniques, keep clearly in mind the process we're creating. Your body will return to natural health and strength if it's given half a chance to heal. When disease strikes, your vital powers merely need "reminding" and encouraging to transform your body back to match the perfect "blueprint" or pattern from which you were originally created.

WEST FACE OF HEALTH AND STRENGTH 125

We could, for the purpose of the point we're investigating, compare this marvelous machine we call the human body to an automobile. An auto is created by artisans from drawings made by designers. If the artisans correctly match the parts and assemblies to the design plan, off the production line comes a good car.

Somewhere in later time and space the car will need repair, either because of normal wear and tear, or because it has been in an accident, or possibly because the owner failed to attend to regular maintenance so that some part wore out.

If the repair is anything more than a simple overhaul and service, mechanics will consult copies of the original design drawings and put matters to rights by rebuilding the necessary parts to the original specifications.

West Face Tide techniques can be influential in performing similar services for your body. Assuming you were born without major defects, you can consider your body to be like the auto we used in the above comparison.

The passing years will almost inevitably take their toll on your muscular strength and the efficiency of your bodily processes. In some exceptional cases this is less evident than for most of us. By some combination of heredity, health care, plain old good luck and an instinctive "tuning in" to West Face Tides, a few people remain almost 100% efficient to advanced ages.

But for the majority of us, unlike Laurence Binyon's heroes in his "Poems for the Fallen," age does indeed weary us, and the years do condemn! The situation is aggravated if we are involved in accidents which damage the body, or if we abuse ourselves by following health-negative habits such as excessive use of alcohol or tobacco, poor dietary intake and general lack of health care.

Take heart! The West Face Tide can act for your body as the most experienced mechanic can for a car, with every imaginable tool and diagnostic instrument at his disposal. By attuning yourself with the West Face energies you can bring your body's performance back up to specification, to perform as your Designer and Creator intended it to be.

126 *WEST FACE OF HEALTH AND STRENGTH*

The basic technique of tuning in to the West Face Tide I've named the *Reverse Time Tableau*. It's simplicity itself, and needs only regular mental efforts and a few minutes of your time each day.

Your focus point, the *Silver Crescent of Apas*, is already set up for you. All you need to add is yourself and your memory.

Sit yourself down where you can see the Silver Crescent. Look at it peacefully for about two minutes then close your eyes.

The objective is to reach out for health and vitality by soaking up energies which allow your body to heal. So approach this mental task by *thinking of yourself as healthy and bursting with energy*.

Most important: do *not* think about your maladies themselves. Thinking to yourself something like, "I wish to heal my sore back," is *not* the way to go. That merely reinforces the idea that you have a sore back, because as you form that sentence in your mind you'll automatically think about your painful and malfunctioning spine. That's a fact: *name* anything, and you at once call up a fleeting mind picture of it, and you most definitely do not want mind pictures of your maladies floating around in the West Face Tide!

Have you got that vital point very clearly in mind? After closing your eyes, case around in your memory for incidents when you were healthy (or at least did not have the maladies that are currently afflicting you). Recall such times, detail by detail.

For instance, think back to when you used to run and jump, dance and exercise. In particular, think about performing tasks and challenges which you now can no longer perform adequately. Note in the case histories included in this Energy Circuit how Eileen, Walter, Beverley and Earl presented the correct mind pictures for the West Face Tide to bring into actuality.

WEST FACE OF HEALTH AND STRENGTH

127

I've called this the *Reverse Time Tableau* because most times your mind pictures will be of yourself in earlier years when you were fitter and stronger. Entertain those thoughts as vividly as possible for a couple of minutes. Then open your eyes, gaze at the Silver Crescent for about ten seconds, and conclude this routine.

What if you're crippled, have been since birth, so that your memory contains no recall of your being fit and totally healthy? Maybe you walk with crutches, and have no clear memory of ever having been able to get about without them. In such a case, use the *Mental Bridge Method*, which is fully described later in this Energy Circuit.

WALTER B. WAS REJUVENATED AND MISTAKEN FOR HIS OWN SON

"I suffered no particular disabiltiy, yet I was growing old too fast," Walter B. said. "At 53 I looked far older. I was low on energy, found exercise debilitating, had lost much of my sex drive, and suffered from back pains. I was much less fit than most men ten years my senior.

"I realized how bad it was when my 64-year-old neighbor and I came out of our homes simultaneously and saw our bus at the end of the street, early for once.

"We both sprinted the 50 yards to the corner to catch it. My neighbor had the extra handicap of the width of his lot, but he overtook me at a gallop and swung aboard the bus in time to tell the driver to "wait for old slowpoke back there." He was hardly breathing heavily, but I had still not recovered when we reached downtown."

While recovering his breath, Walter asked his old neighbor if he had a secret exercise for keeping fit.

"That was how I was introduced to the secret of the *Reverse Time Tableau*," Walter said. "It was all hogwash, I figured. Thinking yourself to fitness? That was too much for

128   *WEST FACE OF HEALTH AND STRENGTH*

me to swallow. Yet the old boy and the bus episode was evidence of something going on."

Almost against his better judgment Walter joined his neighbor in his basement and was shown how to build and decorate his own *New Psychic Energy Generator.*

"I was fair," Walter said. "I gave the *Reverse Time Tableau* a regular workout each day. It was easier than jogging. All I had to do was recall my younger days when I made the baseball team and hit the home run that won us the championship. I did my best to fish around in my memory to recreate that glorious feeling.

"It began to have an effect. I found I could trot up stairs I'd previously toiled up, resting halfway. My wife asked if I'd taken an aphrodisiac as my bedroom energies resurfaced. My graying hair seemed darker and thicker. All kinds of signs of fitness reappeared after years of absence."

Walter finally realized how much he had changed when shopping downtown one day. A young stranger came up to him and greeted him.

"Hi, Johnny," the man said, "I thought you said you'd be out of town for a month."

Walter stared. Johnny was his 27-year-old son, an enthusiastic body-building and fitness buff who was currently on a four-week job-upgrading course in the next state.

"Oops! Sorry," said the stranger. "You're not Johnny. But he never told me he had a brother around his age."

EXPEL PAIN AND SUFFERING WITH THE WESTERN WATER TECHNIQUE

This technique adds an extra healing strength to the foregoing *Reverse Time Tableau.*

Twenty-four hours before performing the *Reverse Time Tableau,* place a container of ordinary drinking water beside your *New Psychic Energy Generator,* on the West Side. The container can be a cup, mug or drinking glass (in which case

WEST FACE OF HEALTH AND STRENGTH

cover it with a piece of paper or card to prevent dust settling into the water). An even better solution is to use a small bottle or vial which you reserve specially for this technique.

Whatever kind of container you use, place it so that it touches the western edge of your *New Psychic Energy Generator*, and leave it undisturbed until you need it.

Carry out the *Reverse Time Tableau* as described above, then when you open your eyes uncover (uncork, uncap) the prepared water and drink it while looking at the *Silver Crescent of Apas*.

Conclude the routine as usual.

By drinking a few ounces of energized liquid prepared with this *Western Water Technique*, you are physically taking into your body the West Face Tide energies, to work at all levels of being to allow your body to attune to healing.

BEVERLEY L. CAN DANCE AGAIN NOW THAT HER VARICOSE VEINS HAVE DISAPPEARED

If you happen to be a close observer of those long-stemmed beauties who dance in chorus lines for our edification, delight and intellectual indulgence, you'll no doubt have admired their smooth and shapely legs.

Beverley L. was one such entertainer, and was seen regularly on television and in theatrical revues. She was also in demand to exhibit her choreographic graces at conventions and stag parties.

"I truly enjoyed my vocation. I was proud to be a chorus girl," Beverley said. "The camaraderie, the smell of the greasepaint, the travel, the applause, the admiring glances when I danced on stage in my briefs and pasties were meat and drink to me.

"Call me a dewy-eyed dreamer if you wish, but my life was the theater, warts and all."

At the peak of her career, just when producers were singling her out for solo dances and the big break seemed just

WEST FACE OF HEALTH AND STRENGTH

around the corner, Beverley began to suffer aches in her legs after standing for a while. She found she had to move her limbs or the pain grew steadily worse.

"That was no good for tableaux and similar statuesque poses," she said, "but I got by without anyone noticing the occasional twitch I made when the discomfort was too much.

"Then blue marks appeared on my legs and thighs, and soon heavy make-up would not totally hide the unsightly blotches."

Worse was to follow. Ugly lumps began to show beneath Beverley's previously smooth and perfect skin. She was developing that scourge of beauty—varicose veins.

"I bleached them, I massaged them, I slept with my legs in the air. I had injections. I took herbal teas alleged to cure them," she said. "They grew steadily worse, more obvious and lumpy every day. Elastic stockings kept them at bay, but eventually my legs looked terrible, especially at the end of a hard day on my feet."

Thus ended her career in the chorus. Beverley could accept engagements only where she could wear slacks or long dresses.

"I was trained as a dancer, and there was precious little other work around for me in show business," she said. "And I had this continual nagging pain that made it difficult to smile on cue. Plus I'd been real proud of my body, and I was ashamed to have to cover it up."

One of the health stores where Beverley bought her herbal teas also sold occult books and psychic assists such as crystal balls and Tarot cards.

"Still looking for a cure for my veins, I asked around the store if anyone knew a witch or wizard who would put a spell on my legs and cure them," Beverley said. "Yes, I was *that* desperate. They laughed and said if there was, they didn't know about it.

"But one of the guys said he knew of a lady who swore Pyramid Energy could do anything, which might even be

WEST FACE OF HEALTH AND STRENGTH

131

true—considering that she lived in luxury and apparently did no work."

Beverley met with the pyramid lady, and poured out her troubles.

"If it can be done, keep up any treatment you're following and add the *Western Water Technique*," she was told.

Since then you'll almost certainly have seen Beverley (that's her real name, not the stage name she uses) on your TV. A few months after she was let into the secrets of Pyramid Energy she was able to resume work with the chorus line.

"Those nasty old veins just shrank and vanished," she said. "I kept a picture of myself in my favorite dancing role, with smooth nylon-clad legs flashing, and my body seemed to catch on and return to that shape. No more pains, either."

A triumphant return to the chorus was soon followed by solo artistry, and starring in a TV series was only a few delighted steps away for Beverley.

"And I took those steps on my new legs," Beverley said. "I'll never know for sure why my varicose veins went away. But they'd been very stubborn until I used the *Western Water Technique*, so I guess we must all reach our own conclusions."

YOUR NATURAL ENERGIES SURGE WHEN YOU USE THE MENTAL BRIDGE METHOD

This method is specially designed for people who are unable to call up clear memories of health and strength. As stated above, this method is to be used in place of the *Reverse Time Tableau* in such special cases.

The method begins exactly the same as the Tableau it replaces, by viewing the Silver Crescent for two minutes and closing your eyes.

Now, instead of fruitlessly seeking memories of your *own* health and strength, spend the next couple of minutes recalling exploits by other people where they were obviously fit and

132 WEST FACE OF HEALTH AND STRENGTH

vital. In particular, "see" those people performing the precise feats which you cannot manage because of your affliction.

If your legs are malfunctioning, recall when you watched a young athlete high-jumping, sprinting or marathon racing. Bringing back memories from a TV program on athletics is ideal for this.

That trick back playing up again? Visualize wrestlers, weightlifters or gymnasts in your exercise.

The mind pictures which show how you wish to be are limited only by your imagination. For example, if your natural energies have been eroded by time or psychological conditions, it's perfectly acceptable to recall an erotic movie as your *Mental Bridge Method* back to perfect function.

Having run your mind pictures for two minutes, open your eyes, view the Silver Crescent for a few seconds and then carry on with your usual routines.

An addition to this method is to also incorporate the *Western Water Technique* as you open your eyes, exactly as described above.

EARL M. REMARRIED, AND FATHERED THREE SONS AT THE AGE OF 78

Earl M. outlived his first wife, and was left a widower at age 72.

"We'd had a good and full life together," he said. "And when the good Lord called her to come home to rest she went with a smile on her face. I know she's waiting for me in the Great Beyond.

"I was feeling the flutter of angels' wings myself and figured it would not be long before I was laid to sleep for eternity beside her mortal remains in the quiet plot we'd reserved so many years before."

But destiny had other plans for Earl before he joined his wife in heaven. Left alone, he found time hung heavy on his hands, and Earl became a regular patron of the mobile library which visited his Iowa village each week.

WEST FACE OF HEALTH AND STRENGTH 133

"I got caught up with psychic discoveries and such strange stuff," he said. "I guess it was a spin-off from thinking about heaven and the unseen worlds. I was amazed to find how many hard-nosed scientists were spending good money on stuff which had not been acceptable in my young days as an engineer.

"I read about moving things with your mind, reading colors with your fingers, divining thoughts at a distance, dream research and a subject that really fascinated me— Pyramid Energy."

Earl eagerly devoured everything he could find on pyramids and wrote away for other information.

"I even got involved in the research myself as best I could," he said. "I set up an experiment to see if the *Mental Bridge Method* could restore my youth. It was so long since I'd felt the sap running I figured that would serve better than the *Reverse Time Tableau*—I had only very hazy memories of the far past."

Earl's mental picture was built around the exploits of James Bond, one of his favorite movie characters. Whenever any TV station ran one of those classic adventures Earl would be glued to the screen.

His experiment was followed by unusual effects.

"I found I was anxious to go to the social club in the village hall," he said. "I had not gone inside there for years. I'd found the men to be talking on subjects that held no interest for me, I never learned cribbage, and those twittering females used to drive me up the wall.

"For the first time in a long, long time I was hankering after female companionship, and not just for tea and cakes, if you understand."

Not long after, Earl was courting a divorcee less than half his age. The whole village was a-twitter at their romance which culminated in marriage.

"Never thought I'd make it to second time around," Earl said, "but here I am, father of two sons and another due next week, or so the doctors say with their newfangled peek-inside-you gadgets.

134 WEST FACE OF HEALTH AND STRENGTH

"I'm 78, feel 35, and reckon to see all three sons produce grandsons for me before I decide to call it quits."

BODILY AND MENTAL PERFECTION CAN FOLLOW THE APPLICATION OF THE SIX-RAYED STAR THOUGHT

So far your full West Face routine, conducted daily when possible, consists of performing the *Reverse Time Tableau* or *Mental Bridge Method*, adding the *Western Water Technique* to either.

To give a final surge of healing energies to whichever routine you adopt, add a final push of vitality to the West Tide with the *Six-Rayed Star Thought.*

As you regard the Silver Crescent and drink the energy-charged water, pretend a six-pointed star is sitting atop your *New Psychic Energy Generator,* sparkling and shining, radiating energy to you.

If you have any trouble thinking of the shape of a six-pointed star, draw two triangles the same size on a piece of paper and cut them out. Put them on the table in front of you, one with a point up, the other with a point down (toward you). Lay one triangle on top of the other. Voila! A six-pointed star!

That's yet another powerful connection to the West Face Tide energies, created by your mind and inserted into the healing equation which will haul you back to blooming vitality and youthfulness.

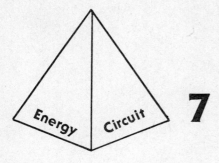

The New Psychic Pyramidic Gestures

Kirlian photography, a method of making pictures of the unseen energy which radiates from people and things, clearly shows that the tips of the human fingers have strong flows of power around them.

This instructive part of our journey to personal power and satisfaction shows you how to use your fingers and hands to harmonize the energies and further open your line of communication with the Cosmic Tides we're employing to bring your desires into material existence.

THESE SECRET GESTURES MAKE NEW PSYCHIC ENERGY POWER FLOW

As we apply *New Psychic Energy Power* to your life, we're operating almost purely in the unseen world, even if the results are apparent in your material spheres. We're lining you up with Tides and currents which we measure not so much by their presence but by their incredible and joyful effects on your life.

136   *NEW PSYCHIC PYRAMIDIC GESTURES*

However, we're most definitely using a physical "door" to the realms where *New Psychic Energy Power* exists, and that's your *New Psychic Energy Generator*. It sits, just like its mighty brothers in Egypt, focusing and directing the Tides of Creation for you, 24 hours a day.

The delightful adjunct to *New Psychic Energy Power* is that you do not have to be in the presence of your Generator to draw on similar life-shaping powers. By applying the form of the pyramid at times when you're out and about, you can create a temporary bridge to call on the pyramid's resistless powers. And one way to build such a bridge is with manual gestures: pyramidal hand shapes which connect you with the Tides when you need them most.

ANNIE D. MADE A LAWYER CHANGE HIS MIND IN HER FAVOR

Annie D. was caught in a closing spiral of bad luck and negativity. Everything she touched crumbled to bitter ashes. In the course of a year she had seen her comfortable world shattered, piece by painful piece.

"I had been a reasonably happy housewife with everything to live for. Now I had turned into a nervous, frightened wreck," she said. "It started when my teenage daughter dropped out of school, ran off with a fat and bearded biker, and fetched up pregnant and addicted to heroin in the Nevada courts.

"My husband drew out most of our savings to go and fetch her back home and on the way back they both died when the car went out of control and flipped into a ravine.

"That left me alone and lonely, with two small girls to raise."

Annie soon ran short on money. Her husband had carried no insurance, and Annie's efforts to find any kind of paying work went no place.

NEW PSYCHIC PYRAMIDIC GESTURES

"Food stamps and welfare helped," she said, "but the bank soon told me they'd be taking our lovely house if I slipped behind in payments, already three months adrift. I clung to our home like crazy, selling the carpets, drapes and furnishings to keep going. I began snapping at my babies, crying myself to sleep after hopelessly walking the empty echoing rooms of the house until late into the night."

Annie's one ray of hope was a legal claim she had launched against the garage which had overhauled the family car. A preliminary police investigation showed a nut and bolt might have worked loose in the steering mechanism, making the car uncontrollable, and thus causing the accident which had deprived Annie of her breadwinner and daughter.

"If I had been able to afford a top lawyer I could have carried the case to the highest courts in the land," Annie said. "It was a fifty-fifty chance, but it seemed I could be awarded damages because of carelessness by the garage.

"But all I could do was to put free legal aid onto it, and although the young lawyer allocated to me did his best, even I could see he was out of his league with the experienced counsel the garage could afford to retain."

Nevertheless Annie's lawyer was able to put together a convincing enough case to have it go forward to trial.

"Counsel for the garage was uncertain enough to invite us to come and talk with them," Annie said. "My lawyer said they were considering offering a cash settlement to save the expense of what could be a long and expensive battle."

The meeting was frightening for Annie. In a somber office she watched as three men talked back and forth, with her future in the balance.

"Our client denies all liability, of course," the lawyer for the garage intoned. "We might, if pressed, be prepared to admit minor contributory negligence, but you would have to prove that to the court's satisfaction.

"This is all off the record, you realize. Our client has authorized us to offer you $1,000 in full and complete settlement provided you agree not to proceed further against him.

138   *NEW PSYCHIC PYRAMIDIC GESTURES*

"In my extensive professional opinion that is more than generous. If you do not accept then we shall let the courts decide, and you realize that can take years, and you could get nothing at all."

Annie let her lawyer do the talking. A thousand dollars was precious little in exchange for the loss of a husband and daughter, she thought. She had hoped for enough to save her home and provide some over to live on until she could get on her feet again.

The lawyers wrangled on. The garage representative grudgingly advanced the offer to $1,500. Annie's lawyer continued to press for more.

"This is getting us nowhere," said the garage lawyer with finality. "We had best terminate this time-wasting. We shall see you in court when a date has been set, and we will fight you every inch of the way."

Annie felt the chill of fear clutch her heart. Any delay meant she would lose her home, and where she would take her children was a dreadful question mark.

"I recalled a good luck sign my old aunt used to use when she was in trouble," Annie said. "She said she learned it from a mysterious man she met in Cairo, Egypt, and she relied on its powers to ease her life.

"Under the table I pointed my finger at the garage lawyer and made a triangle movement, then curled my finger and thumb together."

Annie's lawyer was presenting a last-ditch rebuttal as she did this. Her lawyer's eloquence was interrupted as a young man entered the office and whispered in the garage lawyer's ear. The man stood up, excused himself and left the room.

He returned a few minutes later. His previous triumphant smile was strained.

"My client desires us to reach a settlement before we part," he said. "Can we still reach a satisfactory compromise?"

Knowing there must a very good reason for this sudden change of heart, Annie's lawyer moved in like a champ. He

NEW PSYCHIC PYRAMIDIC GESTURES

began airily talking of the heavy damages, in the hundreds of thousands, which he would proceed to sue for.

"I thought it was sheer bravado," Annie said. "I was amazed to see the garage lawyers put their heads together solemnly to discuss their next response."

The legal hassling was hot and heavy for the next hour and much of it was way over Annie's head. Finally her lawyer pressed a pen into her trembling hand and told her to sign a paper.

"All I could see was the figure of $550,000," she said. "Not until I banked the check, paid off the mortgage and began drawing $3,000 a month interest from the balance did I believe I was free and clear.

"What had happened was that a police report had been released that conclusively proved the garage to be at fault. The representing lawyer knew the report would be presented as evidence and his client no longer had any hope of winning the case. The lawyer had to make a quick decision and keep his client's losses to a minimum—so that meant more than half a million dollars in my purse."

Annie is happier now. The loss of her husband and daughter is still keen, but she is able to live in comfort, and is being courted by a doctor, with future marriage a distinct possibility.

"Who knows if that good luck sign had any effect?" Annie said. "Strange how everything changed after I made it."

The gesture Annie made at the crucial stage in the interview was the *Digital Triad Gesture* next described.

THE SIMPLE DIGITAL TRIAD GESTURE

You'll probably recognize part of this hand gesture. Throughout the ages, mystics, theurgists and priests have recognized the power of this "hand pyramid" which brings the Tides to your aid at times of need.

NEW PSYCHIC PYRAMIDIC GESTURES

Point the first finger of the hand you normally use for writing, with your thumb and other three fingers curled loosely into your palm. This is the instinctive gesture of "pointing" we use when we wish to turn someone's attention to some point in space.

Now move the tip of your finger around an imaginary triangle, as if you were following the outline of the *Scarlet Triangle of Tejas*. Start at the bottom left corner, move your fingertip up and to the right to the apex, then down to the bottom righthand corner, finally moving the fingertip left, back to its starting point.

Having completed that small and unobtrusive movement, put your first and second fingers together (same hand), and touch them to the tip of your thumb. Your third and fourth fingers are still curled into your palm.

Your forefinger and thumb now form a rough letter "O." Hold this gesture for about ten seconds.

Those two apparently minor movements of the hand and fingers put your mental and physical energy flows in tune with Cosmic Tides. The next case history shows another amazing sequence which occurred when the *Digital Triad Gesture* was employed as a protective sign.

JOSEPH H. MADE THE DIGITAL TRIAD GESTURE AND SURVIVED A CATASTROPHE

A thousand feet of empty space yawned below Joseph H. as he clung to a rock face. Icy winds whipped at his body, flattened against the sheer mountain. Between Joseph and a swift fall into the jaws of death lay only the security of a slim rope and his climbing expertise.

"Hazardous, yes," he said, "but only part of mountaineering. The sheer thrill of inching up a difficult peak, finding crevices to support hands and feet, using muscle and wits to overcome adversity was unmatched stimulation for me."

NEW PSYCHIC PYRAMIDIC GESTURES

Joseph's companion waved from a broad ledge some 50 feet above.

"He'd driven a piton into a crack and secured the rope to it," Joseph said. "That iron spike would support me as I climbed."

That was the plan, but the mountain had other ideas. As Joseph put strain on the rope preparatory to ascending, the apparently solid rock, rotted by frost below the surface, suddenly crumbled and split. The piton flew free, a shower of stones and gravel descended on Joseph, and the rope fell past him, snaking out loose and useless to aid him.

"I had a precarious foothold on a two-inch ledge," Joseph said. "One hand held a knob of rock, but I needed the leverage of a rope to raise me to the next handhold. And with that fall of rock I realized any part of the cliff could crumble under my fingers.

"Without a rope to save me I'd have about eight seconds to say my prayers before smashing to oblivion on the cruel rocks far below."

Joseph's companion peered down, horrified, as he hurriedly uncoiled a spare rope. Joseph's strained expression on his upturned face showed he could not cling on much longer. Could the rope be dropped to him and secured before he plunged to his death?

"Cramps began in my arm, quivering under the strain of holding me against the overhang," Joseph related. "I needed a higher point to grip with my other hand. If I could manage that, I could see a slim chance of making it to the ledge above. But the rock under my hand felt smooth, with no gripping surface.

"Ridiculous what you do when all seems lost. I recalled a sign of safety and salvation a friend of mine in the ministry had told me would save my soul. That was about all it looked as though I could save—even as my companion above was hammering in another spike for the new rope I felt my hold weakening."

NEW PSYCHIC PYRAMIDIC GESTURES

Prepared now to give his life as the forfeit in his hopeless contest with the mountain, Joseph moved his fingers in the age-old gesture.

"I glanced at my hand as I made the final circle with thumb and finger," he said, "and through that little circle I saw a slim crack in the rock face which my groping hand had missed. It was the chance I needed. Slipping my fingers into the tiny crevice I hauled myself higher, praying the rock was sound."

Minutes later a shaken Joseph stood beside his companion on the ledge.

"The exhilaration was indescribable," Joseph said. "One moment I was doomed, and then hope had returned and I reached comparative safety.

"I would be dead today if I had not seen that crack in the rock."

As you will have realized, the sign Joseph made which foiled death was the *Digital Triad Gesture*.

THE QUARTET OF PROTECTION AND MIRACLES

By grouping together the four energy fields which exist at the tips of your fingers, you create a highly protective and inspirational condition.

This gesture is not unlike the second part of the *Digital Triad Gesture*, but it adds two more fingers to the hand shape. A second difference is that you use the opposite hand to the one with which you perform the *Digital Triad Gesture*.

Hold out your hand, palm up. Left hand for right-handed people; right hand for lefties. Move your first and fourth fingers toward each other until they touch near their tips. Bring your second and third fingers together and touch the nail of your forefinger with your second finger and the nail of your fourth finger with your third finger.

Try this as you read it. It's not half as complicated as it sounds!

NEW PSYCHIC PYRAMIDIC GESTURES **143**

Curl this clump of four fingers over slightly toward the palm, then press the pad of your thumb onto the tops of the four fingers so that your thumb is in contact with all four.

Hold the *Quartet of Protection and Miracles* gesture for ten seconds or so.

FACING CERTAIN DISASTER, TAMARA F. USED THE QUARTET OF PROTECTION AND MIRACLES AND LIVED

"A terrible feeling of helplessness sweeps over you when you know you're in a crippled aircraft and your life depends on the skill and luck of one man at the controls," Tamara F. relates. "I found the truth of that firsthand."

Tamara was a passenger in a chartered twin-engine Cessna, battling rain, fog and high winds thousands of feet above the Rocky Mountains.

"We five passengers clung white-knuckled to our seats as the little craft bucked and swayed," Tamara said. "Up front the pilot was outwardly calm but tight-lipped. He'd seen the danger signs of an overheating engine on his instrument panel and was nursing his fuel, aiming for a landing strip about 100 miles distant."

A flickering glare suddenly lit the cabin, turning the surrounding fog a swirling, eddying blood red. The starboard engine was burning fiercely.

"Safety procedures," the pilot shouted, "I'm taking us down."

As the nose dipped sickeningly, Tamara strapped herself in and crouched forward as instructed. She knew only too well the statistics: despite all safety precautions, when an aircraft crashes a high proportion of the crew and passengers do not survive.

"I felt a sickening lurch and a sharp scraping and tearing as we touched the tips of pine trees on a bluff. The pilot was battling to put us down on a flat area he could glimpse through the mist in a valley straight ahead," Tamara

144   *NEW PSYCHIC PYRAMIDIC GESTURES*

said. "We needed heavenly protection and a miracle to get us down and clear of the burning wreck. In the last moments before we hit, I felt ice cold. With an instinctive hand movement I built the *Quartet of Protection and Miracles*, a Pyramid Energy gesture I had learned but had never had to use."

Tamara says they hit the ground surprisingly gently.

"It was no worse a jolt than being in a minor car collision," she said. "Then we were sliding fast across the wet ground, with pieces of burning wreckage and flaming fuel eddying high in the air. With a groan of tortured metal the redhot engine tore free and dropped behind, flaring angrily.

"Careening and swaying, we slowed. The horrible crunching faded and died. For a moment there was a chilling silence, then someone cheered. The applause was picked up by the rest of the passengers as the pilot waved us to silence. 'Sorry about that,' he said, 'I've made better landings in my time. Let's get out of here.'"

Lights bobbed in the distance. Help was already on the way as Tamara and her fellow travelers climbed from the little wreck which had threatened to be their coffin. Far across the scrubland the engine still flared fitfully, guiding the rescuers.

"They were amazed to find no one even scratched," Tamara said. "We were able to use the ambulance as a bus to take us to the warmth and welcome of a nearby ski resort.

"The investigators who later combed the wreckage reported our survival as a small miracle of skilled piloting and a major miracle of protective destiny. Did the *Quartet of Protection and Miracles* have something to do with it? I'll never know for sure—but I'll repeat it if I'm ever in such danger again."

WHAT CAN YOUR NEW PSYCHIC ENERGY GESTURES DO FOR YOU?

You need all the help you can get in your search for the bridge of attunement between the world of material form and the unseen world of energies, destiny and fate.

NEW PSYCHIC PYRAMIDIC GESTURES 145

New Psychic Energy Gestures are part of the help this book offers. As you make the described hand shapes, so you alter the energy flows of your body, throwing a kind of psychic "fishing line" into the Tides around you. And what you "catch" depends on what you need at that time for maximum harmony, fulfillment or safety.

Used at the right times (although I hasten to add there are no strictly "wrong" times to use such helpful gestures) your *New Psychic Energy Gestures* will help to bring to pass the event you desire, provided that event is in your best interests of safety, freedom from want and joyful survival.

The Gestures will work on particular requests or on a non-specific, intangible circumstance. They are, in fact, best at manipulating the latter: "danger" is often a very abstract concept, but the Gestures will unerringly protect you from it and its worst effects.

The all-encompassing answer to the question in the headline above is, "Anything you need is yours when you use the *New Psychic Energy Gestures*."

"I NEVER THOUGHT THEY WERE THAT POWERFUL," WRITES WALDO U.

Waldo U., who (not surprisingly) uses a different name on the covers of the books he writes, had a peculiar problem. He deeply desired to help people who were calling on him for aid, yet he was going broke in the process, in a manner he had never foreseen when he became a professional author some five years earlier.

"The writer of any book hopes his readers will write to him. Their letters help him to write better books which fill stated needs," Waldo said. "When you write an instructional book you expect some people will write for clarifcation when the words in print are less expressive than they should have been.

"When I began writing fulltime I vowed I would spend time on a personal reply to every letter that came in, provided I could read the writing and understand the contents."

NEW PSYCHIC PYRAMIDIC GESTURES

Little did he know the Pandora's box he'd opened. In poured veritable mountains of mail soon after his first book was in the stores.

"I tried," Waldo said. "God knows I tried. I wrote far into the night and sent off sacks of answers. Some of those brought further letters, pages and pages long, requesting further correspondence. It seems some authors solve the problem by ignoring all letters, and I had become a rare source of free information.

"I had to call a temporary halt when my second book was running behind schedule because I was spending too much time on personal letters. But when my accountant went over my books at year-end, I had a further shock.

"Some readers believe when they buy a book that the author gets their check or cash as his reward. Not true: such people forget that the printer, the typesetter, the binder, the paper manufacturer and all the other skilled people involved in creating a book have to be paid by the publisher, who also has offices to maintain, a staff to pay and overhead to meet.

"Most times with average sales, if a book costs $9, the publisher needs $8.55 of that for production costs, and the author gets the remaining 45 cents. That's why all authors except the few top-flight best-sellers also work at other jobs to make a living.

"So every reader who wrote to me had paid me just 45 cents, and wanted my time, paper and mailing charges as an extra on top of the contents of the book. I had replied the best I knew how, using paper and envelopes costing about five cents, plus a stamp. On top of that I'd had to allocate at least 20 minutes of my time to compose and type the reply. Even at minimum wage, it was costing me about $1.30 to try to satisfy one reader, and I'd replied to about 3,000 during the preceding year—$3,900 laid out in exchange for a received $1,350.

"That's the kind of economics to put any person in the poorhouse. My accountant flatly forbade me to do it, unless I was prepared to go broke."

NEW PSYCHIC PYRAMIDIC GESTURES

Waldo was concerned. He still wished to satisfy readers who had questions, but he could not afford the time and money to reply to them.

"Obviously I needed a miracle. A colleague of mine suggested—seriously or not, I'm not sure—that I make the *Quartet of Protection and Miracles* over the pile of mail as it arrived each morning," Waldo said. "If it promised to help, I was game to give it a try."

Since writing two more books, Waldo's mail deliveries have grown heavier, not lighter, so he is still unable to answer all his letters.

"I read and enjoy them," he said. "I use them to write new books which fill gaps I unintentionally left in previous efforts. I believe my readers understand a busy author has much more mail than he can possibly handle, and they're not too upset if theirs is not one of the lucky ones that get a reply."

Waldo reports an amazing change in his mail since he began making the Quartet over it.

"I used to find a self-addressed stamped envelope in about one in ten letters," he said. "Most times I could not use it because I live in a country other than that of many of my readers. So I still had to use a stamp from the country I was in when I replied.

"The change was that some four to ten readers began sticking a quarter to their letters to help with the mailing charges. And although few people know about them, other correspondents were enclosing International Reply Coupons which all post offices sell, and which I can exchange for local stamps.

"That still did not reimburse me for my time, but it made life much easier. Naturally, the letters with enclosed postage went to the top of the reply-pending heap, even if it did take me weeks to get to some of them—for there were literally hundreds, I'm pleased to say!

"Maybe that all sounds like a tempest in a teacup to you, but to me it was a true miracle. I could keep more of my

148 *NEW PSYCHIC PYRAMIDIC GESTURES*

readers satisfied without going into bankruptcy in the process. I never thought the Gestures could be so powerful, but they've made me happy, and even my accountant gave his grudging assent!"

WHEN TO USE YOUR NEW PSYCHIC ENERGY GESTURES

When should you use your New Psychic Energy Gestures?

Whenever you feel your mental or physical energy levels are below par. Whenever you need to ensure your *New Psychic Energy Power* routines are making maximum contact with the Cosmic Tides. Whenever you need a little extra help, vitality, inspiration, success or direction.

Consider them partly as extras; options you add to your already powerful Tide Techniques to bring success more quickly and gloriously. Making either of the *New Psychic Energy Gestures* for a few seconds while you conclude a routine, or while actually performing that routine, adds to the force and harmony you're creating.

But consider them also as strong self-contained mystic tools. Note in the case histories how Annie, Joseph and Tamara used them appropriately to gain major advantages.

MARY J. HAS EVERYTHING SHE NEEDS, THANKS TO NEW PSYCHIC ENERGY GESTURES

Mary J. is a firm believer in all types of psychic and mental self-help methods. She has a small library of different books that bring health, wealth and happiness in unseen and unusual ways.

"Friends ask me why I have so many books," she says. "They say if I have one method of making my life happy and harmonious, why do I not stick to it alone?

NEW PSYCHIC PYRAMIDIC GESTURES

"I have found it best in my personal case to slowly evolve my unique techniques, incorporating different routines which I've found work best for me. Any book has to aim at a wide audience, and very few people will be able to say they're 100 per cent successful, instantly, with any one procedure, whether it's psychic power, magic, prayer or whatever.

"I have also discovered, probably for astrological reasons, that a method will work well for me at one time and yet be less fortunate a month later. That's when I move over to different techniques to bring my desires into my environment."

Whatever technique Mary is using at any time, she attests to the universal assistance of *New Psychic Energy Gestures*.

"Possibly because they've been used by adepts for centuries," she said, "they fit to any technique, magical or mundane.

"Since I have added them to my happiness-producing routines I can feel the extra boost they give to the powers. I gladly affirm I have everything I've ever needed, and in great measure that's thanks to *New Psychic Energy Gestures*."

ALL TECHNIQUES ARE IMPROVED BY ADDING NEW PSYCHIC ENERGY GESTURES

You should know that these *New Psychic Energy Gestures* are universal in application. Whether you're using only this book to find your dreams come true, or whether you're incorporating other methods and studying different techniques, your *New Psychic Energy Gestures* will add extra power to whatever you're attempting.

Even mundane work will go easier. The *Digital Triad Gesture* is used by many people I know as a sure and precise aid to memory.

A well-known metaphysical teacher in the U.S. uses the *Digital Triad Gesture* when he's lecturing. His audiences are

150   *NEW PSYCHIC PYRAMIDIC GESTURES*

invariably amazed at his total recall. Point by point he covers his subject, stating facts and figures, names and places as if he had a script in front of him. But it's all spoken from memory, and he gives his secret to his inner circle of graduate students.

Herewith that secret, which is not copyrighted or new: you can see the gesture being used by subjects in many religious paintings dating back centuries!

When you're at a loss for a fact, a subject or any piece of data, make the *Digital Triad Gesture*, and at once the needed words will be at the front of your mind. It's that simple. Try it!

A successful British author (who wishes to remain anonymous) makes the *Quartet of Protection and Miracles* as he sits down at his typewriter.

"Ideas and plots at once flow into my mind," he says. "I've tried writing without making the Quartet, and find words then come only slowly. The instant I connect the right energy currents with the Gesture, the concepts I need practically write themselves!"

Not only mind work comes easier with the Gestures. Paul V. makes furniture, and uses both Gestures at intervals while working.

"Whenever I hit a difficult patch I make one of the gestures, and the solution comes at once," he said. "My tools almost seem to guide themselves."

And having learned those valuable Gestures, read on to Energy Circuit 8 where you add more powerful shapes to your arsenal of pyramid weapons to shape fate the way you wish it to be.

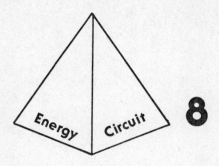

Your Three Facial Psychic Pyramidic Features

Nature and your Creator knew about the power of pyramids long before researchers stumbled over the vast resources of these energies which exist in conjunction with solids made up of a square and four triangles. But it may come as a surprise to you to learn that you were born with the power of the pyramid and other mystic symbols as features of your face and head.

This Energy Circuit investigates how you can find and use these powerful features to best effect.

NATURE HAS GIVEN YOU THREE PRIME NEW PSYCHIC ENERGY FEATURES

Right on the front of your face are three *New Psychic Energy Features,* each carrying its awesome ability to align you with the life-gladdening Cosmic Tides. Especially in manipulating human relationships and day-to-day events by focusing the fields of energy which exist in front of your face and brain, you can literally make people do what you want.

151

152   THREE FACIAL PSYCHIC PYRAMIDIC FEATURES

RUDOLF E. "THOUGHT IT WAS STUPID"
BUT CHANGED HIS MIND WHEN MIRACLES
HAPPENED TO HIM

Rudolf E. signed up for a lecture on pyramid energy only because his girlfriend said she'd go alone if he was not interested.

"You can appreciate my attitude of mind when you realize I signed the entry form 'Rudolf E., Skeptic' and figured I'd thrown the lecture fee down a particularly useless drain," Rudolf said. "I went along with the express intention of scoffing and jeering about that freaky pyramid stuff."

However, Rudolf behaved reasonably well at the lecture, asking penetrating questions about the validity of the Pyramid Energy concept.

"I was surprised at how much genuine scientific effort had gone into investigating the mysteries of pyramids," he said. "Although still denying there was anything in it, I had to allow some good brains seemed to believe they were on to something.

"Afterward I spoke to the lecturer. He was pleased to enlarge on the subject, and suggested I give the techniques a fair chance before dismissing them."

Rudolf, a fair though stubborn man, agreed.

"If I could personally see results which would not normally have taken place without pyramid techniques I was prepared to be more positive about them," he said. "The lecturer singled out *New Psychic Energy Features* as being useful to my proof. He did not call them by that name at the time: that title was evolved later, but the techniques were identical to later methods."

Rudolf made a private joke of the *New Psychic Energy Features* with his girlfriend. He said he expected and wished them to fail so he could say "Told you so!" Yet he was soon forced to admit life events were swinging his way.

THREE FACIAL PSYCHIC PYRAMIDIC FEATURES 153

"I kept careful notes," he said. "I would write down my expectations of the outcome of an event, and then record the actual result. If the results were consistently better than expected, I'd have to grant Pyramid Energy some of the credit.

"I'm an electronic engineer and I often come up against design problems which defeat me for ages. It usually takes many trials and errors before finding satisfactory solutions. In three specific cases I recorded, I expected each to take several days to overcome. The tasks were to remove "bugs" from a client's security system.

"After employing *New Psychic Energy Feature* routines, the right solution to each problem flashed into my mind, and they worked first time."

Rudolf earned praise and promotion for that inspired effort for his employer.

"On another occasion I was called in to explain to a very obdurate client why he would have to pay $200,000 for a gizmo when he'd been expecting it would cost around $10,000," Rudolf recalls. "All the best sales people had tried their persuasion, while managers and other engineers had argued without success. When I entered the picture my prognostication was that we were about to lose a large order.

"Another step toward management followed for me after the client not only agreed that the price was fair but also doubled his order! *New Psychic Energy Features* were proving out well."

Lofted into the heady and opulent surroundings of top executive, Rudolf found himself called upon to do much of his work by telephone.

"That's not always the easiest way to get things done, since it lacks the personal touch," Rudolf said, "but *New Psychic Energy Features* were equal to it. My department gained a reputation for being the most productive and efficient, ahead of all others. I put it down to my newfound ability to unsnarl logjams when persuading people to change their

154   *THREE FACIAL PSYCHIC PYRAMIDIC FEATURES*

minds in our favor even though they were thousands of miles away."

Rudolf has stamped a confident "CASE PROVEN" on his *New Psychic Energy Features* notebook.

"I thought it was stupid when I started," he said, "but some happenings have been true miracles. *New Psychic Energy Features* are my willing servants and tools from now on."

YOUR RHINAL ENERGY FOCUS

The most prominent pyramid-shaped feature of any face, one which you can hardly miss when you know about it, is your nose. Its pyramid shape is obvious once you look at it, with your nostrils forming the side of the base, and the bridge of your nose, right between your eyes, forming the apex.

From those three points streams a composite flow of never-ending energy, and once you know how you can direct that energy in unseen ways which will bring you advantages and progress.

We can identify this source as your *Rhinal Energy Focus*, and I'll be telling you how to employ its titanic force after we've looked at your other two *Psychic Energy Features*.

"I'M MILES AHEAD SINCE USING MY RHINAL ENERGY FOCUS REGULARLY," WRITES JANE O.

"I work for a collection agency," Jane O. said. "My job is to track down people who skip town, leaving debts behind them.

"I do the locating and then hand over to the collectors. You cannot collect from someone who's walked away from money owing if you have no idea of his or her whereabouts, so my work is vital to the operation of part of our organization."

THREE FACIAL PSYCHIC PYRAMIDIC FEATURES   155

Jane's income is dependent on her degree of success in finding people who have reasons to try to stay out of sight. She is paid a small percentage of any money recovered, so she has to be on her toes to stay solvent.

"You need to be something of a detective," Jane said. "Most cases are fairly simple because the debtor may disappear but leave his family and stay in touch with them. A little deception, which I feel is justified when someone else's money is being deliberately withheld, often leads direct to the culprit.

"Stickier cases are those where the debtor is almost a professional conperson. He or she moves to an area, gets a job, establishes credit and gradually runs up heavy debts. Then they skip, perhaps to another country, or right across the continent. Computers are making it more difficult, but it's still possible to disappear and resurface with a new identity."

Jane encountered Pyramid Energy the same way many others have—by reading a book about it. She wondered if she could use its powers in her work, to improve a slump she was in which was hurting her life style.

"The *Rhinal Energy Focus* offered an interesting promise," Jane said. "I began to use it when faced with apparently insoluble disappearances.

"My technique was to apply the energy, then ask myself, 'If I was the debtor, where would I go and what would I do?' In many cases I found answers popping into my mind, sometimes including place names, that I would never have reached logically."

Typically, Jane corraled a hardcore skipper after her *Rhinal Energy Focus* had her zero in on the man's possible location.

"I had much unrelated data about him, but could not put it together," she said. "My *Rhinal Energy Focus* tied together my knowledge that he could swim well, was something of a show-off and loved the ladies, was proud of his health and strength, hated snow, loved working in the open air, and would be unlikely to have left the country because of certain problems he'd had with the police.

156   *THREE FACIAL PSYCHIC PYRAMIDIC FEATURES*

"California came to mind, then life-saving. A little checking with the authorities showed that a man answering the description had been employed as a lifeguard since shortly after my 'mark' disappeared from Texas. A different name and a faked work history did not stop me from nailing him, sequestering his salary and putting a lien on his possessions."

Jane's new Porsche sportscar is one visible sign that her slump is behind her. She has acquired the reputation of being "the girl who always gets her man." She enjoys the challenge of all the bigger and more difficult cases.

"No more dull routine traces for me," she said. "I'm miles ahead of my colleagues. Better run for cover if you're thinking of skipping—my *Rhinal Energy Focus* will 'nose' you out in no time!"

YOUR OPTIC-GLOSSAL ENERGY FOCUS

Some psychics will tell you they can actually see rods of psychic force streaming from your eyes. The undeniable power of those twin streams is a basic clue to the existence of a second *New Psychic Energy Feature* pyramid shape on your face.

Note the position of your mouth and lips in relation to your eyes. They form a triangle, with the apex down (your mouth) and the horizontal baseline bounded by your eyes, one at each end.

The spoken word, which entails exhaling breath from your lungs through your mouth, has traditional powers recognized in all occult disciplines. Thus you can easily understand how your *Optic-Glossal Energy Focus*, created from your eyes and mouth, is the combined source of intermingled metaphysical energies.

Properly directed, this Energy Focus is truly startling in its effects, as Tom W. witnesses in the following case history.

THREE FACIAL PSYCHIC PYRAMIDIC FEATURES **157**

TOM W. TRIPLED HIS SALES AFTER LEARNING ABOUT HIS OPTIC-GLOSSAL ENERGY FOCUS

Not to put too fine a point on it, Tom W. was a terrible salesman. While his colleagues pulled down a good living, Tom only just met his minimum targets. He trembled every-time the sales manager spoke to him, feeling sure he was due to be let go for his poor performance. He was wrong, but he came close.

"I'm keeping you on because I believe you can do it, Tom," the sales manager told him one day. "You've got all the right attributes and background to make you a top-flight seller, yet you close fewer deals than anyone else on the team.

"I can give you until September 30 to smarten up. I'll talk to you then."

Tom had two brief months to turn failure into success. He worked on commission only, and his recent poor sales record had made him feel the pinch.

"My charge cards were loaded to the limit," he said, "that's how many commission people cross the inevitable flat patches in their sales. Then when things improve they pay off their debts and the credit cards are ready for use in the next slack period. I'd been in such a slack period for almost a year, and if I failed to improve it was no job, no car, no apartment, no nothing for me."

Casting around for sales techniques, Tom happened upon the *Optic-Glossal Energy Focus*, having exhausted the resources of orthodox sales-assist techniques.

"We can keep this short," he said, "We have to because I've got four people clamoring to buy from me today. My selling sky-rocketed, and clients just lay down to buy. The first week I made more deals than I'd closed in the previous two months.

"When it came time for me to talk to the sales manager I could hold my head high. He patted me on the back and gave me a bonus. I'd tripled my sales, they're still on an upcurve,

158 THREE FACIAL PSYCHIC PYRAMIDIC FEATURES

and I'm leading contender for the cash bonus for top sales-person this year.

"The *Optic-Glossal Energy Focus* started this miracle and no one's more thankful than I am."

LOCATING YOUR INVISIBLE MANDIBLE-PINEAL ENERGY FOCUS

Probing even more deeply into the unseen realms of the Cosmic Tides, we're going to locate your third *New Psychic Energy Feature*, one which is hidden within your skull. Its firm connection with the source of much psychic activity, your pineal gland, explains part of the name of this *Mandible-Pineal Energy Focus*.

Your pineal gland is itself cone-shaped—a modified pyramid shape we'll be investigating in Energy Circuit 10. The pineal is at the base of your brain, at the top of your spinal column, almost centered in your skull just above eye level.

It was known to the ancients as the "seat of the soul," and is also the 'Third Eye' of mystery and inspiration mentioned in almost all esoteric teachings. And certainly medical science has yet to find anything physical which the pineal does for the body, so it may well be that its sole purpose is to focus psychic energies.

Your pineal gland forms the apex of your triangular *Mandible-Pineal Energy Focus*, and the two points of the base of this focus are to be found along your jawbone.

Put your fingertips on your cheeks and tuck your thumbs under your jaw on either side, just below your ears. Move your thumbs forward around the curve of the underside of your jawbone, feeling the shape of the lower side of the bone by gently pushing your thumbs into your neck.

> *NOTE: The key word is "gently." Important arteries run up to your brain in the area you're feeling with your thumbs. Excess pressure could cause fainting.*

THREE FACIAL PSYCHIC PYRAMIDIC FEATURES **159**

About an inch or so in front of your ears you'll feel a kind of "kink" or minor arch in the bone. These are your mandible points of this Energy Focus.

The spot is unmistakable once you've located it on either side of your jaw. Press your thumb on the bone (*not* into your neck) and rock it forward and backward. You'll be able to distinctly feel the cavity in your jawbone.

Thus we have the three points located: one in your forehead between your eyes and about an inch above your eyebrows. That's the pineal point. And the left and right mandible points are those in your jaw which we've just established.

SUE B. WOKE UP PROFITABLE PERSONAL POWERS BY USING HER MANDIBLE-PINEAL ENERGY FOCUS

Sue B. had always been shy and retiring. A strict and rigid father had squashed her personality, and when she grew to adulthood she instinctively treated all people as if they were like her parent.

"Even though I consciously knew the attitude was false, my subconscious approach to people, especially males, assumed they were going to slap me down," she said. "I could not open up to living my life to the full. 'You're no good, you're stupid and you can't do anything' admonitions echoed across the years, carved into my personality from childhood.

"Thus I backed off from situations where I might have proven my worth, and gained a rightful reputation for being a colorless mouse with no backbone."

Recognizing her problem was one thing, curing it quite another.

"Frustrations piled up, directed against myself," Sue said. "Try as I might, I could not bring myself to move forward and speak up in my behalf. People walked all over my rights

160 THREE FACIAL PSYCHIC PYRAMIDIC FEATURES

and I stayed dumbly in the background, battling with unresolved fears."

Sue's life deteriorated, and she began to wonder if perhaps she was indeed stupid and useless.

"I married a beautiful man and we had three children," she said. "I guess I was happy enough, especially after I withdrew into a fantasy world where I was not required to relate to anyone except my family. My husband was a brilliant man who easily accomplished anything he set his mind to, which did little good for my fumbling attempts to gain self-confidence. He never took the trouble to find out what made me tick, assuming I was self-effacing from choice.

"Only I knew the turmoil inside me, as I longed to use my abilities to reach a better self-image."

The children grew up and left home to marry and pursue careers. Sue and her husband dropped into a regular and apparently comfortable routine.

"We had a fine home, with all the material comforts you could ask for, money in the bank and a peaceful relationship," Sue said. "No one realized, and I was not about to enlighten them, that I was bored, bored, bored! Within me I longed for something fresh, something new and exciting—yet I did not know what it was I needed!"

During the long winter evenings beside their crackling log fire Sue emulated her husband, an avid reader. She combed the public library and after exhausting the fiction shelves she began to pick and choose from the non-fiction, learning about subjects she had never before encountered.

"After I had dabbled in astrology, biology, chemistry, divination and you-name-it on through the rest of the alphabet, Pyramid Energy caught my imagination," Sue said. "I bugged the librarian to get me everything possible on pyramids, from the archeology of Egypt to the latest psychic research reports."

Her initial interest grew into an enthusiastic pursuit of data on pyramids.

"The interaction of ductless glands and psychic energies

THREE FACIAL PSYCHIC PYRAMIDIC FEATURES   161

which stems from Eastern philosophies led me to the concept of the *Mandible-Pineal Energy Focus*," Sue said.[1] "By trial and error I discovered what a magnificent assist it can be to visualizing and achieving life goals."

Sue's researches brought her in contact with many other people of like mind and interests.

"When I took stock of my life I suddenly found I had come out of my shell," she said. "I'd uncovered a consuming interest and my self-doubts had vanished.

"My initial pyramid research spread into other areas of psychic energy. I tapped a resource of creativity I was unaware existed within me, and took up oil painting and writing a book. I began traveling to lecture on psychic powers, and the world beat a path to my door to show me I was not the useless person I used to think I was."

Sue and her husband have moved up in the world. Her new interests also sparked his involvement. Their future plans include cooperating on new books on the use of psychic energies and allied fields.

"I'm earning money for myself now," Sue said, "which is most satisfying. I've also ceased lecturing because I found it tedious—but having withdrawn again from the world to some extent, this time it's on my own terms. The alteration in my personal outlook is a miracle which I firmly attribute to Pyramid Energy."

MAKING FULL USE OF YOUR FACIAL NEW PSYCHIC ENERGY FEATURES

We have identified three potent triangles of force. Your nose forms your *Rhinal Energy Focus*. Your mouth and eyes make up the *Optic-Glossal Energy Focus*. Your "Third Eye"

---

[1]The names "Rhinal Energy Focus," "Optic-Glossal Energy Focus" and "Mandible-Pineal Energy Focus" were evolved by Sue B. She has graciously permitted me to use them, and I gladly acknowledge the aid I have received from her in formulating this section of this book.—*Geof Gray-Cobb.*

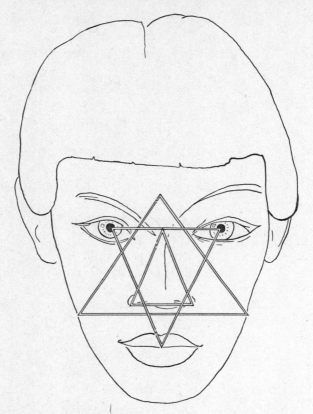

FIGURE 5: Combined New Psychic Energy Features

or pineal gland behind your forehead and the mandible points on each side of your jaw make up the triangle of your *Mandible-Pineal Energy Focus*.

Notice the powerful and mystic shape the three of those would sketch on your face if they were visible to the naked eye. Remember the *Six-Rayed Star Thought* you added to your *New Psychic Energy Generator* in Energy Circuit 6? That powerful symbol is formed by your *Optic-Glossal* and *Mandible-Pineal Energy Focuses*, while your *Rhinal Energy Focus* sits firmly in the center of this facial Six-Rayed Star. Figure 5 shows what I'm telling you, and it's a helpful picture to keep in mind during your daily routines.

THREE FACIAL PSYCHIC PYRAMIDIC FEATURES

163

Directed by your thoughts and actions, this mental symbol of protection and power is ready to help with creating any miracle you'd like to name that can ease your path during your life affairs.

Using Your Rhinal Energy Focus

Consider this as your psychic assist to answering insoluble questions and solving mysteries, working automatically for you and offering valuable answers and advice.

By considering any problem and then running your attention around your *Rhinal Energy Focus* you connect yourself with sources of wisdom which are usually closed to your conscious, decision-making mind. The solution to what is bothering you appears accurately and clearly in your mind, and all you have to do is act on the information received. Result is another mystery solved, another question answered, and another giant step taken toward personal harmony, peace of mind and fulfillment.

Prime obstacles to using this startling source of Cosmic Wisdom are your own opinions, biases and beliefs. Your *Rhinal Energy Focus* can offer a valuable and valid solution to a problem, yet you'll ignore it, thinking you know better.

So you need to somehow "switch off" your conscious mind where your logic exists, and let Cosmic Wisdom approach your problem through intuition and pure inspiration.

But how do you persuade your conscious mind to stop muddying the pool of the bright penetrating light of inspiration? How do you stop it interfering with this vital decision-making process?

Simple: let your *Rhinal Energy Focus* work while you're sleeping. At that time your conscious mind is dormant, and your subconscious predominates. Under those conditions your *Rhinal Energy Focus* can hit peak efficiency.

While you're creating your *Akashic List of Desires and Needs*—an exciting concept you will be introduced to in Energy Circuit 11—you'll be able to identify the problems and

164   *THREE FACIAL PSYCHIC PYRAMIDIC FEATURES*

questions which can be solved by sharp and inspired inputs from yourself.

That's exactly what your *Rhinal Energy Focus* is for. So set up the best conditions for it to do its invaluable work.

Put a pad and pencil on the night table beside your bed. On the first page of the pad write your major question which needs an answer as soon as possible.

As you drift into sleep, deliberately think about that question. As soon as you've mentally stated it, think about your *Rhinal Energy Focus*, running your attention around it. Think about your right nostril, then your left nostril, finally the bridge of your nose. As you do this simple mind exercise, feel the air you breathe flowing into your nasal cavities.

> *NOTE: Disregard that last if you have a sinus problem, or if there's any other reason why you're unable to nose-breathe.*

That's the first step. Drift off to sleep and enjoy your dreams.

The second step comes when you wake up. Even before your eyes are fully open, reach out for the pad and pencil and scribble down the first thing that comes into your head. Do not wait until you're fully awake, or your conscious mind will interfere with the inspiration.

The third step comes later. After you're properly awake and have a few minutes to spare, sit down with your pad and review your question of the previous night and see what your *Rhinal Energy Focus* has suggested as a solution. That will be contained in the sleepy scrawl which you made as you were waking.

The fourth and final step is to *act* on that Cosmic Advice, provided it will not physically hurt anyone or break any laws.

Using Your Optic-Glossal Energy Focus

Most of the more important events in your life occur face to face with other people. Your *Optic-Glossal Energy Focus* is

THREE FACIAL PSYCHIC PYRAMIDIC FEATURES 165

custom-created to give you the edge over the opposition in any such confrontation.

Whenever you're talking to someone (or you are being talked at!) you can use your *Optic-Glossal Energy Focus* to shape the outcome of the conversation, discussion, argument or statement to your total and complete advantage.

What you're going to do is to direct the power of *your Optic-Glossal Energy Focus* into your opposite number's *Rhinal Energy Focus*! Thus your thoughts, desires and needs will *by-pass* the conscious mind of the person you are talking to and sweep unerringly deep into his or her subconscious mind. At that level any of your opponent's hang-ups about you, stubborn resistance and prejudices toward you or the situation are taken out of the picture. The decisions he is *forced* to make are based purely on what is best for *you*!

The process is easy. You're going to *look* at the bridge of the person's nose as you're conversing, and also *speak* toward that same spot.

Caution, please! First and foremost, you should not make a big production out of this, otherwise your opponent will get the idea you're spooky or freaky. If you stare like a basilisk all the time, you'll probably prevent the technique from working properly.

And when I suggest you talk to your opponent's nose, I do *not* mean that you should lean forward and talk to it as if you were addressing the ear of a deaf person.

The more unobtrusive you are with this technique, the better it will work. There's no need to fix your gaze on the person's nose and hold it throughout.

Make it much more casual than that. When you meet and greet each other, make sure you look at the person's nose, directly between the eyes. Briefly will do fine. Also be sure, when you speak your opening sentences, that your mouth is turned toward your opponent.

At intervals during the exchange, reinforce the process by glancing at his or her nose, and turning your face so your words are heading toward the same spot.

And if you run into one of those situations where your

166   THREE FACIAL PSYCHIC PYRAMIDIC FEATURES

opponent says, "I'll have to think about it. We'll let you know later," be sure as you say goodbye that your closing words and gaze are sent directly at your interviewer's *Rhinal Energy Focus* apex.

Using Your Invisible Mandible-Pineal Energy Focus

We have investigated your *Optic-Glossal Energy Focus* and seen how to use it in face-to-face situations. But what if the encounter consists of dealing with a person who is not in the same room as yourself?

For instance, Alexander Graham Bell is responsible for much of our conversation being carried on at long distance, where you are unable to see your opposite number as you talk.

Obviously you cannot effectively employ your *Optic-Glossal Energy Focus.* So this is where your *Mandible-Pineal Energy Focus* comes into its own.

Its energy is activated very handily. Touching either of (or both) your mandible points with your thumb, or your pineal point with your fourth finger, is sufficient to add the enormous persuasive and manipulative power of this Energy Focus to the situation.

When using the telephone it's simplicity itself to tuck your thumb under your jawbone and switch on the energy by feeling your mandible point. To add to the efficiency of the process you can tuck the thumb of your free hand under your other mandible point, spread your hand across your face and touch the pineal point with your little finger.

This last can be a trifle difficult if you wear glasses or have a long face and a small hand. If your reach is insufficient, just touch your little finger to the middle of your forehead.

This activation of your *Mandible-Pineal Energy Focus* is

THREE FACIAL PSYCHIC PYRAMIDIC FEATURES   167

amazingly effective in both small and large life situations. I used it myself at this precise stage of writing this book.

My long-suffering electric typewriter had developed a major mechanical fault. I took it to the repair store and explained that I needed it repaired most urgently. A technician looked it over, made that frown and pursed-lips expression which always heralds bad news, and opined that he might be able to repair it within ten days . . . two weeks for sure.

There was no real problem. He loaned me a free replacement machine to use until my typewriter was repaired. I went home again.

Next day, writing these words about the *Mandible-Pineal Energy Focus* on the borrowed typewriter, I decided I'd give the technique a workout for experimental proof.

I called the repair store, holding my telephone as I've described above, activating my right mandible point with my thumb. I explained to a lady at the store that it would be nice if they could hurry my typewriter repair. She promised to call me back in an hour.

Right on the dot of 60 minutes later my telephone rang.

"You can come and pick up your machine any time after 1:00 p.m. today," the technician told me.

I did that and the words began flowing again from my familiar typewriter instead of from the stranger which had so briefly occupied my desk.

One application of the *Mandible-Pineal Energy Focus* had reduced an estimated ten *days* for the repair to less than five *hours!*

But influencing people is only one of the exciting uses to which you can put your *Mandible-Pineal Energy Focus*. Merely by considering a desired result, you can bring it to pass.

Read next how Saul P. used his *Mandible-Pineal Energy Focus* to swing destiny his way and achieve his most cherished desires. You can do likewise!

"THE FACIAL NEW PSYCHIC ENERGY FEATURES KNOWLEDGE HAS TRANSFORMED THE QUALITY OF MY LIFE," SAYS SAUL P.

If you live within sight of the sea on the West Coast of America or Canada you will almost certainly have watched in awe and amazement a super-opulent white cruising ship pass along the horizon, ablaze with lights. On the lighted decks, in dance halls, bars and private suites, leisured revellers disport. Bands play lively tunes, the pool echoes to gay laughter and white-clad flunkies are everywhere, carrying trays of food and drink at the beckon of bejewelled fingers.

Out there on the ocean glides the good life, and chances are you're unknowingly watching part of Saul P.'s empire of leisure in action. Saul himself may well be lounging in one of the satin-lined cabins with every luxury devised by human ingenuity at his fingertips, not excluding the slimmest, most beautiful and cooperative ladies money can buy.

"Born to wealth? Not on your life," Saul says. "I was an abandoned illegitimate child, dragged up—it was too rough to call it raised—in foster homes and welfare hostels. My schooling was not much; I played hookey in the sixth grade and never went back.

"Before I was 20 I'd seen the inside of a dozen jail cells for transgressions ranging from vagrancy to illegal possession. I was an outcast, living on my wits on the wrong side of the law. Stealing cars became my way of getting from one city to the next, and knocking over pharmacies, stores and motels provided my income.

"Not the life I'd have chosen if I had my druthers, but I knew nothing different or better."

Saul was aware there were strata of society where wealth and ease ruled supreme, but his aspirations hardly went beyond vague plans of stealing a millionaire's wallet if he had the opportunity.

THREE FACIAL PSYCHIC PYRAMIDIC FEATURES 169

Broke and hungry (an occupational hazard for Saul), he was casing a store in New Orleans where his wanderings had taken him.

"It was an easy touch," he said. "One old guy running it, very few customers and the right amount of people on the street—not too many to get in the way, but enough to get lost among. No big deal, but all routine and simple and good for about $200."

Confidently Saul walked into the store, holding a folded newspaper over his hand. He thrust it forward as the old man shuffled toward him.

"Stand right there and keep still," Saul said quietly. "There's a gun under this paper and I'll use it if I have to."

Saul had no gun, but the bluff rarely failed. Saul eased around the counter, heading for the cash drawer, keeping an eye on the old man.

The drawer opened easily and Saul began stuffing bills in his jacket pocket. All went smoothly. The man watched Saul, but made no move. Saul took the last of the cash and moved toward the door.

"If you'd like to stay healthy, forget you saw me," Saul said. "Don't make a move until I've been gone five minutes. I'll be watching."

Saul was startled when the old man smiled.

"Good luck to you, my son," the old man said. "A favor you could do me. It might save others from undergoing such an indignity as this. It could give you a new outlook on life. Take that book on the counter there and at your leisure, read it."

Saul knew from experience that the less a hold-up victim is upset, the better chances the robber has of getting clean away before the alarms go off. Purely to humor the old man— "Nutty as fruitcake," Saul thought—he picked up the book and stuffed it in his pocket as he backed out of the store, turned and hurried into the anonymity of sidestreets.

"I found I'd ripped off nearly $250," Saul said. "The book I figured must be a religious tract. I also figured God

170   *THREE FACIAL PSYCHIC PYRAMIDIC FEATURES*

had given up on me long before, so being saved was not my trip.

"I was surprised to find the book was on Pyramid Energy, something I'd never heard of. I needed to lie low in case my description was on the street, so I hung around in my room, reading the book. Stumbling through it, more like, but even a slow reader like me found most of it easy to understand, and some of the ideas were too far out to be possible— or so I thought."

Even though some of the words in the book might as well have been in Sanskrit for all the meaning they had to him, Saul picked up enough to start using his Facial Energy Focuses. At first he visualized himself as brilliantly successful with his crimes.

"No effect," Saul said. "I was ready to call it quits and garbage when I recalled the author had said Pyramid Energy would work only positively. I was trying to use it to break the law.

"Strange, but the fact it did *not* work, just as the author said, kind of convinced me he might be telling it like it was.

"So for the first time in my life I tried a thing called the *Mandible-Pineal Energy Focus* to help me. Shoot! I could hardly say those 64-dollar words, but I sure found I could *use* them!"

Saul's change from his squalid life of petty crime to a life in the lap of platinum-plated luxury was as quick as it was startling to him.

"First a guy in a bar offered me a job! A straight, cash-on-the-barrelhead perfectly legal employment ferrying cars across the country," Saul related. "That was something new for me. It took me quickly to a partnership in a small car dealership. We struck lucky when an import we were handling ran away with the small car trade for a while. We made a minor fortune, selling the business to a bigger outfit for mucho bucks before the bottom dropped out of that market.

"I got the Midas touch. Everything I touched turned to gold. On a hunch I bought some Canadian mine stocks at a

THREE FACIAL PSYCHIC PYRAMIDIC FEATURES   171

dime each and they shot up to $15. The $2,000 I'd invested put $291,000 in my bank when I sold. That windfall set me up for really big dealing and I could do no wrong."

We looked at Saul's present position at the beginning of this case history. What we did not see was his penthouse in New York for which he paid a cool $3,000,000, his mountain retreat in Oregon, his incredible estate in Louisiana where he converted an old mansion with electronics and space-age technology to a dream of air-conditioned convenience. Neither did we see his helicopter, private zoo, 18 automobiles both ancient and modern, gambling casino and private airport.

"There's much more, but some of my most precious possessions no one can ever see," Saul said. "Pyramid Energy brought me happiness, freedom and security, priceless things I'd never known before.

"A funny postscript, by the way. I went back to see that old man I robbed. I reckoned I owed him about a million.

"Would you believe he was still smiling, and would take just the $250 I'd taken off him, plus $4.95 for the book? He said that made us square—the rest of the profit was mine, because I'd done all the work! That kind of work is nice if you can get it, and anyone can if he tunes in to Pyramid Energy."

**YOUR FACIAL NEW PSYCHIC ENERGY
FEATURES WILL WORK FOR YOU 24 HOURS
EACH AND EVERY DAY**

You now know about the three triangular pyramid Energy Focuses which you can call on any time to help you improve your life.

Once you've put them into action, they'll continue to work for you all the time. Waking or sleeping, even when you're not thinking about directing their powers, they'll be shaping your future toward the most delightful conditions imaginable.

172 THREE FACIAL PSYCHIC PYRAMIDIC FEATURES

The act of connecting your personal hotline to the Cosmic Tides is something like opening a long-closed door. The energies start to flow, then continue to flow, adding more and more positivity to your existence, sculpting your destiny into glory on a fulltime basis.

One useful piece of advice regarding these energies is that you should try to arrange your mundane routines to cooperate with the Tides.

As a simple "for instance," you may be lonely and seeking friends. Having called the Tides to your aid, make sure you move into areas where you're *likely* to meet new people.

Granted you could sit locked away in your room, and eventually destiny would shape up your future so new friends came calling. You can reduce the waiting time by a significant percentage by doing your part: in the planes of the unseen, destiny and the Tides work to bring your desires true and will pick up on any chain of events which produces the desired result. In the material planes, you can do your bit to *shorten* that chain of events by deliberately inserting fair chances of your desires coming true into your future.

Consider that point carefully: you and destiny can make an irresistible team with *both* of you operating in harmony at your individual levels of being.

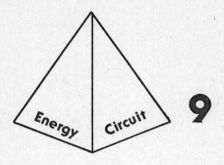

The New Psychic Pyramidic Healing Postures

Here we add yet another powerful technique to your battery of tuning-in processes which allow the Cosmic Tides to sweep you joyfully to a new and better life.

This Energy Circuit incorporates more pyramid shapes into the picture, to aid your West Face tuning-in methods as you aspire to, and achieve, the vitality and glorious experience of perfect health.

The idea presented is that as you use your *New Psychic Energy Generator* to align your body with healing energies, so you physically arrange your limbs to make pyramid postures which further amplify the power and feed it directly to the areas where your body needs most aid in curing itself.

HOW TO COMBINE THESE POSTURES WITH WEST FACE TECHNIQUES

If you're truly serious about healing your body (and you

174 NEW PSYCHIC PYRAMIDIC HEALING POSTURES

should be if you wish to fully enjoy all the other bounties the Cosmic Tides will bring you), then *New Psychic Energy Healing Postures* should be combined with the West Face techniques explained in Energy Circuit 6.

The basic instructions are simple. As you perform the West Face techniques, arrange your body and limbs in the comfortable positions I'm about to describe. This may take a little moving around in your working space adjacent to your *New Psychic Energy Generator*.

For example, when you work in the posture of the *Pedal-Patella Healing Triad*, you need to be lying flat on your back with your knees up. While explaining the positions to you in detail, I leave it to you to arrange your position and sight lines to fulfill the basic requirements for viewing your *New Psychic Energy Generator*.

And right here in this book is where some of my more uncertain and despairing readers will feel abandoned and neglected by me. Earlier I promised step-by-step instructions, and now I'm telling you to figure something out for yourself!

Here's why. I have not walked away and left you to struggle on your own again, but one thing I must avoid is to totally "spoon feed" you in this book. Some details must be left for you to work out for yourself.

For instance, I could have written at length on exactly how to place your *New Psychic Energy Generator* so that you can best view all your faces when required. With a purpose, I have laid the responsibility on you to work out such bits of routine business.

You understand this is a course of tuning yourself to Cosmic Tides of energy, and I have repeatedly suggested that your involvement, in your own way, using your energy, time and thought is absolutely essential to success.

So any situation you set up incorporating your unique solution to any problem puts your personal stamp on the tuning-in process. Thus you custom tailor your mind and body more quickly.

NEW PSYCHIC PYRAMIDIC HEALING POSTURES **175**

PREVIOUSLY SPASTIC AND APPARENTLY RETARDED EDIE M. NOW LEADS A NORMAL LIFE

"Our daughter Edie is a special child," writes Mrs. M. of New Jersey. "A drug prescribed for me during pregnancy resulted in her being born spastic, apparently retarded.

"Her disabilities prevented her from moving her feet and arms properly; she was unable to feed or dress herself; she could not speak distinctly; and she made frequent grimaces and jerky, purposeless movements."

Edie was given the best medical care possible. A complete diagnostic examination advised treatment which included muscle re-education as part of the therapy.

"She was put on a program of relaxation, practice of voluntary muscle control and development of proper movement patterns," reports Mrs. M. "She was also given speech therapy."

Mr. and Mrs. M., strong believers in Pyramid Energy, encouraged the child to include the *Pedal-Patella Healing Triad* in her exercises.

"We must be careful to report only what we know occurred," Mrs. M. states, "laying no specific claims to any particular routine.

"Edie is now 14 years old, able to eat tidily, tie her shoes unaided, speak with only a slight problem with sibilants, and her tics and jerks are minimal.

"Compared with the sad state she was in five years ago, she now leads a normal life. Her doctors are delighted with her progress and anticipate that by the time she has completed high school she will be indistinguishable from any other average teenager."

THE PEDAL-PATELLA HEALING TRIAD

The *Pedal-Patella Healing Triad* arranges your body to

176   *NEW PSYCHIC PYRAMIDIC HEALING POSTURES*

create a solid and powerful pyramid with the lower trunk and limbs.

Lie flat on your back with your legs together. If you're lying on the floor, put a pillow or other pad under you buttocks and another cushion under your head. If you can arrange yourself north and south, with your head pointing to the north, so much the better—but this is neither essential nor critical to this routine.

Keeping your legs together, raise your knees and put your feet flat on the floor. Move your feet toward your buttocks as far as you can *without straining any muscles.* Take it slow and easy and stop the movement the moment any tendon complains!

Now edge your feet apart about 12 inches or so, until by raising your head you can see your heels as you look past the curve of your hip. Keep your knees touching each other, fold your hands comfortably across your chest until you need to move them, and you're in the *Pedal-Patella Healing Triad* posture.

"I CAN NOW LIFT 200 POUNDS," ATTESTS ACCIDENT VICTIM MEL A.

Being bedridden was literally agony for Mel A. When a steel beam fell on him in an industrial accident, he sustained a fractured pelvis and a compound fracture of the left femur.

"Despite existing in a fog of pain-killing drugs, it was painful to stir," he reports, "but the worst of the pain was mental. I'd always been athletic, regularly working out on the beams and lifting weights. To lie there not knowing whether I'd ever again run or walk without a limp was the true torture."

Released from hospital, Mel began the long fight back to health. Eventually he was able to walk, but slowly and painfully. His physician encouraged him to exercise muscles which had become flabby while he was on his back.

NEW PSYCHIC PYRAMIDIC HEALING POSTURES   177

"Regular X-rays showed the broken bones were knitting," Mel said, "but so slowly I could have screamed with impatience at times.

"The gentle calisthenics I was allowed to do initially were frustrating. I had very little strength and even less endurance at the outset."

A friend Mel met while swimming at the Y related how he employed the *Pedal-Patella Healing Triad* whenever he was suffering from anything from a wrenched tendon to a hangnail.

"Seemed harmless enough," Mel said. "Useless, too, yet it certainly would not do me any damage to try it. I strongly doubted my friend's enthusiastic claims, but agreed to include in my daily workout the version of the West Face technique he laid on me."

Mel records his recovery was rapid thereafter. "Maybe my body was ready to heal," he said. "Or maybe there is something in that Pyramid Energy stuff after all. Why sit in judgment? My personal marvel is that I can sprint, do gymnastics, and clean and jerk 200 pounds. That would hardly get me into the Olympics, but it's ten pounds better than I could lift before my accident."

THE FINGER CONTACT TONUS TECHNIQUE

Sitting, standing, kneeling, lying—you can adopt this *Finger Contact Tonus Technique* in any bodily position as long as your hands are free to touch each other.

In a manner akin to the way an acupuncturist alters the energy flows of the body with his needles, this hand posture balances metaphysical energies to help your West Face techniques reach quicker attunement with natural healing powers.

I'm about to describe how to place your fingers, but this is a clear case where one picture is worth a thousand words.

FIGURE 6: Finger Contact Tonus Technique

Look at Figure 6 and you'll see how to place your hands to achieve the *Finger Contact Tonus Technique*.

Hold your hands a few inches apart, palms facing. Hold your fingers straight, and keep them all as straight as feasible throughout.

Move your hands together until you can touch the tips of your thumbs together, and the tips of your little (fourth) fingers likewise.

Place the tip of your left forefinger against the tip of your right *second* finger.

Then place the tip of your left second finger to the tip of your right *third* finger.

You now have two fingers left over which are not touching their tips to other fingers. They are the third finger of your left hand, and the forefinger of your right hand.

Swing these two fingers down to touch the *base* of their opposite number on the other hand—your right forefinger touches the base of your left forefinger, and your left third finger touches the base of your right third finger.

Straighten out any fingers which you may have bent while putting this together. Check against Figure 6 to see

NEW PSYCHIC PYRAMIDIC HEALING POSTURES   179

you've got it right. This is your *Finger Contact Tonus Technique.*

CHRONIC MALADIES LEFT AFTER MARILYN H. TRIED THE FINGER CONTACT TONUS TECHNIQUE

When she gave birth to a baby on June 1, the birthday of movie star Marilyn Monroe, an Ohio woman named her child after the Hollywood leading lady, hoping her daughter might grow up to be as beautiful, famous and wealthy as her namesake.

That was more than a decade before Marilyn Monroe died so tragically, after her classic rags-to-riches rise to stardom.

"Looking back on it, I began to go downhill after Miss Monroe died in 1962," said Marilyn H., "I was 12 at the time and recall the shock wave that went around the world when everyone's favorite pin-up was found so mysteriously dead.

"As my mother hoped, I had been showing some grace and formative beauty up till then—or so my parents say, and their snapshots of me confirm it. Yet within a couple of years that had all changed."

Marilyn H. fell prey to acne and sinus conditions. She developed an embarrassing twitch of the face which made her shy of meeting new people and situations. Asthma appeared in her early teens.

"Dizzy spells and migraines added themselves to my misery," Marilyn said. "Painful menstruation had been with me since my periods began."

Her life became a circuit of doctor to doctor, clinic to clinic, specialist to specialist.

"Temporary relief was all I got," she said. "I was literally sick of my body. Each week a new prescription, hope for a cure, then back to the familiar discomfort and inconvenience.

180 NEW PSYCHIC PYRAMIDIC HEALING POSTURES

My kidneys also began playing up so that I could never move more than a few yards from a restroom.

"I was truly wretched and could not enjoy anything like a normal social life. And the biggest frustration was that the physicians could find no organic cause for any of my sickness."

Marilyn began to try less orthodox treatments.

"Naturopaths sold me tinctures. Chiropractors manipulated my spine. Faith healers laid their hands on me," she recalls. "I even tried hypnosis, but I went to an amateur instead of a clinical hypnotherapist. All he did was seduce me while I was under his influence. He said it was vital therapy for me. It may have temporarily solved his problem, but it did nothing for me."

Heading for a nervous breakdown with her symptoms worsening, Marilyn turned to herbs, organic foods and nature cures.

"They were marginally effective," she said, "and while I was following all of those treatments—except that I'd given up on hypnosis!—the manager of an organic food store introduced me to Pyramid Energy."

Willing to clutch at any straw by then, Marilyn set up a daily routine of pyramid work.

"West Face techniques were my prime involvement," she said, "and I added the *Finger Contact Tonus Technique.*

"It took a while, but from the outset I felt hope stirring. I first achieved greater relaxation and acceptance of my condition. Some of my hopelessness fell away, and the asthma, migraines and dizziness were less prominent."

Her maladies receded slowly but surely. Now in her late 30's, Marilyn still keeps up her pyramid routines.

"I'm radiantly healthy today," she reports. "All the chronic conditions I'd endured so long have left me. I have found a splendid balance of mental and physical energies, and at times when everyone around me is going down with colds and fever, I'm the one who stays well.

NEW PSYCHIC PYRAMIDIC HEALING POSTURES 181

"What a difference from the years before Pyramid Energy came into my life."

THE CRANIAL COVER NEW PSYCHIC ENERGY CIRCUIT

When a doctor takes an EEG (electroencephalogram) of a patient, he is recording electrical impulses and changes in the brain which show up as electrical energy patterns on the surface of the skull.

This Healing Posture connects those same brain energy patterns to important life flows in the palms and fingers of your hands. The resulting interchange of energies can bring lasting harmony to out-of-kilter bodily processes. This reinforces your plan to attune with the West Face Tide and help your physical body heal itself of any malfunctions.

Even more valuable, this Posture can steady down wavering or disturbed mental conditions.

Put your hands over your ears, fingers pointing upward, as you might if you were trying to shut out a loud noise. Slide your hands upward, fingers spread wide, curling them over to keep close contact with your head.

Stop moving your hands as soon as any fingers of your left and right hands touch. The most likely pair to touch first will be your third fingers.

Keeping your palms stationary, make slight adjustments to your fingers until your third and fourth fingers are touching their opposite numbers on the other hand. By all means move your palms a trifle to achieve this double contact, but make the movement as small as possible.

Flatten all fingers firmly onto your head, feeling a warm contact from all fingers and your palms. Swing your elbows forward until they are about four inches apart.

Again, no straining, please. If your physical condition means you have to strain to reach any position I spell out,

182 NEW PSYCHIC PYRAMIDIC HEALING POSTURES

stop before you reach any pain threshold from complaining muscles or joints.

Hold that pose. Close your eyes for about 30 seconds, breathing easily and naturally.

That is your *Cranial Cover New Psychic Energy Circuit* posture.

"THEY SAID I WAS DUMB," WRITES DICK W., "BUT THE CRANIAL COVER NEW PSYCHIC ENERGY CIRCUIT HELPED TO ALTER THAT"

Dick W. suffered from nerves and neuroses. He was, in the vernacular, afraid of his own shadow. Vague and tenuous fears of disaster haunted him and he felt a malignant destiny was against him.

"I spent more time peering into dark corners of my mind to keep unseen devils at bay than I did studying," he recalled. "My parents had me checked out by the best medical experts and they said there was no physical cause for my complexes. Mental therapy was advised."

By the time he was admitted to a psychiatric clinic as an outpatient, Dick was a nervous wreck. At 23 he was hearing noises in his head, faint and indecipherable.

"I felt the distant noises were important to my welfare," he said. "I was convinced that if I could hear what they were, I would receive great revelations. They were present most of the time, so I was constantly distracted from normal social exchanges, unable to put consecutive thoughts together because I had to stop thinking and listen to my inner sounds."

Dick's long silences and preoccupation turned his friends off. He was treated as if he were retarded, and found himself isolated in loneliness, unable to communicate with anyone.

"The most polite epithet applied to me was 'dumb'. Less flattering appellations implied I was a moron," he said. "I had

NEW PSYCHIC PYRAMIDIC HEALING POSTURES

not lost my marbles: all I wanted was some clarity and explanation of why I was the way I was."

While Dick was undergoing therapy, his psychiatrist tried hard to find some area of normal life which would interest his patient. If Dick could be distracted from his "voices" there was a good chance they would fade and disappear.

"After I'd been through a dozen hobbies and recreations and lost interest in all of them my doctor tried something more unorthodox," Dick said. "I was obsessed with what was going on deep within my mind, so he deliberately turned my attention that way. He said if I'd had the education he'd have had me enroll in a psychology class. As it was we had to find something less academic."

Psychic research was the answer, even though the doctor had reservations about it. He knew unguided dabbling with certain areas of the subject can cause increased disorientation and mental disturbances.

"To steer me around that potential hazard he had me read up on Pyramid Energy," Dick said. "He told me at least that was based on scientific facts even if he was intellectually doubtful of some of the claims of the pyramid exponents."

Dick admits he began his pyramid routines with the express intention of amplifying his inner sounds. He was still convinced of their veracity, and needed to hear a meaning within them.

"The technique now named the *Cranial Cover New Psychic Energy Circuit* was followed by unexpected success," Dick reports. "To my initial disappointment my inner voices began to fade and appear only irregularly. Soon they were audible only at full moon. Then they ceased.

"Result was I lost my introverted stance and became interested in the world outside my head. I took up my studies again, continued with therapy to resolve my new emerging personality, and became a new person."

Today Dick is a successful executive, well adjusted to society, normal in every way.

DETECTING THE FLOW OF NEW PSYCHIC ENERGY POWER

While the most obvious evidence of your attunement with the Cosmic Tides and the flow of *New Psychic Energy Power* is the fascinating and wonderful changes which take place in your life, some readers will need more proof to convince them that these metaphysical energies and flows are not mere imagination, wishful thinking and mystical tomfoolery.

Try this experiment. What you're going to do is distort or bend your natural force field by physical means. When you remove the warp and your force field returns to its regular pattern, you will feel undeniable physical evidence of this reversal of your *New Psychic Energy Power* flow.

Stand sideways about 12 inches from any wall of a room. Press the back of your hand, your forearm and your elbow flat against the wall. Do not *lean* on the arm: pushing against the wall with the flat of your arm is the idea.

Continue that push for a slow count of 20. Then step away from the wall.

At once you'll feel a growing lightness in your arm. If you allow it to, your arm will lift upward. And notice it does not lift sideways as you might expect if this were a muscle reaction to the release of the stress. No—your arm rises up in front of you, *parallel* to where the wall was when you were pushing.

This strange phenomenon illustrates your personal force field returning to normal. Even the most skeptical will have to admit the existence of this sensation.

SANDY A. ZOOMED FROM WELFARE TO WEALTH

"When you're disoriented and physically below par it's hard to get ahead," Sandy A. says. "My life on welfare was no picnic, but no way could I fight my way out of the pit I was in."

NEW PSYCHIC PYRAMIDIC HEALING POSTURES   185

Sandy is a product of the "flower children" generation. Her experiences in Haight Ashbury, deep in the hippie culture, had left their mark physically, the results of malnutrition, social diseases and hepatitis. Her mental scars are invisible, but no less real. Experiments with mind-altering drugs culminating in heroin addiction have made continuing therapy necessary.

"I'm no longer on heroin," Sandy said, "but I know I could be again, all too easily. Like once you've been hooked and apparently cured you find your mind offering all kinds of convincing reasons why just one more fix will do no harm."

Uneducated, unkempt, unwanted and averse to taking work in "straight" society, Sandy inevitably slid into poverty.

"Welfare keeps your body alive," she said, "but only *you* can keep your mind active. I had slipped into a morbid detachment, convinced the world had no place where I could fit in and be contented. I ate, drank, went to the bathroom, washed occasionally, watched TV, wandered the streets, and stared at the wall. My only social involvement was occasional sex with casual acquaintances. That was purely a physical need without meaningful exchanges.

"I had no friends and no future. Life was so drab I even lacked the motivation to end it with suicide."

As you may have anticipated, knowing the object of this case history, Pyramid Energy came into Sandy's sad life.

"It began as a put-on in a bar where I'd been taken by a guy I met on the street," she said. "He showed me a tiny pyramid he'd made and carried on his keyring. A neat piece of work, hand carved and painted.

"He stood it beside my glass and said that the little chip of plastic contained the answers to the Mysteries of the Universe."

Sandy was intrigued despite herself, and wanted to know more. Her companion was willing, and in following days showed her many pyramid routines.

"I moved in with him," she said. "I was surprised at how wealthy he really was, even though he looked like any other jeans-and-beads layabout."

186 *NEW PSYCHIC PYRAMIDIC HEALING POSTURES*

The unobtrusive opulence opened welcoming arms to encompass Sandy. Without any deliberate intention on her part she found herself smartening up.

"Life was stimulating," she said, "and I soon found myself managing a small boutique my mentor set me up in."

From there Sandy zoomed to wealth. She now owns a chain of exclusive boutiques nationwide, and the fashions her highly paid designers create now clothe the bodies of high society matrons and rising starlets alike.

"Although money and luxuries came automatically," Sandy said, "most of all I enjoy the sense of achievement. That's something money cannot buy. In my humble opinion, tuning in to Pyramid Energy is better than owning all the gold in Fort Knox."

WHEN TO ADOPT YOUR NEW PSYCHIC ENERGY HEALING POSTURES

You've been shown three Healing Postures: the *Pedal-Patella Healing Triad*, the *Finger Contact Tonus Technique*, and the *Cranial Cover New Psychic Energy Circuit*.

Although they all help you to harmonize with West Face Tide energies and to help heal all ailments, they have specific applications where their startling forces are even more efficiently deployed.

Using the Pedal-Patella Healing Triad

This brings healing energies flowing to your body, especially along arms, legs and the spine.

You'll find the Healing Triad most effective when you're undergoing treatment for a sore back, strained major muscles, pain in ankle, knee, hip, shoulder, elbow or wrist joints, and malfunctions of internal organs.

By and large, use the Healing Triad in work on major physical defects and maladies.

NEW PSYCHIC PYRAMIDIC HEALING POSTURES

Using the Finger Contact Tonus Technique

This energy attunement lifts depression, especially physical depletion which has allowed germ or virus infections to gain a hold in your body.

So influenza, the common cold, fevers and non-specific virus invasions respond well to the Tonus Technique when used in conjunction with the West Face techniques described in Energy Circuit 6.

Using the Cranial Cover New Psychic Energy Circuit

This radiant technique operates at mental and even more ethereal levels. It's excellent for removing general "mind fuzziness" and bringing clarity to confused thinking patterns.

It's also a whiz at helping to alleviate occasional headaches. But severe or persistent headaches should be taken to your doctor at once, with the Cranial Cover used in private as an assist to advised treatment.

Most cogently, if you're told that your malady "is all in your mind" let the *Cranial Cover New Psychic Energy Circuit* move in and you can experience blessed relief.

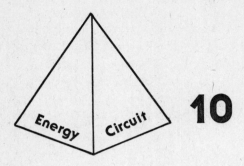

THE AMAZING NEW PSYCHIC PYRAMIDIC CONE

Imagine a pyramid made of rubber or flexible plastic sheets. By some means we begin to curve the sides outward, making the pyramid fat and less angular. If we finally bend each side into a quarter-circle, we would find we have a circular "pyramid" instead of a square one.

That new shape is, of course, a cone—and researchers are finding that any cone, as a specialized pyramid shape, also carries its own invisible energies and power fields which can work changes in the material world which defy logical scientific analysis.

THE NEW PSYCHIC ENERGY CONE FOCUSES A SPECIALIZED FORM OF METAPHYSICAL POWER

I have debated long and hard before including this Energy Circuit in this book. Much research has still to be done to establish exactly where the cone shape fits into the scheme of Cosmic Energies.

AMAZING NEW PSYCHIC PYRAMIDIC CONE

However I believe in offering you, the reader, every possible chance to get ahead, and the Cone most definitely has worked incredibly well for some people.

So in keeping with my philosophy that if something helps to bring harmony it should receive the widest possible publicity, I offer this Energy Circuit as a new and stimulating technique which will help some people.

I fully realize this *New Psychic Energy Cone* technique may not work miracles for everyone. On the other hand, no one can come to any harm using the Cone energies, and some of you will receive outstanding results.

Treat this Energy Circuit as a foretaste of metaphysical concepts of the future. Cone energies may well prove to be the next logical step beyond Pyramid Energies. You can thus see yourself as one of the Wrights or Curies of metaphysical research, experimenting with very new and yet-to-be-understood techniques which could form the basics of a whole new psychic science.

Certainly, based on the evidence which is in so far, the Cone uses a specialized form of metaphysical power which has different effects to Pyramid Energies, and could conceivably replace it for personal miracle working.

"I WAS UNSURE WHAT TO DO," SAYS LEW B. "THE NEW PSYCHIC ENERGY CONE AUTOMATICALLY BROUGHT ME HAPPINESS"

Passing a few empty hours by reading a paperback on the power of pyramids, Lew B. smiled at the report of how a housewife avoided surgery by sitting over a cone until she found her hemorrhoids shrinking.

"I needed a cure for constipation, not piles," Lew said. "But not a blockage in my bowels. What I could not get moving was my head."

Lew had reached a plateau in his life where he could not figure out what his best move should be.

190 AMAZING NEW PSYCHIC PYRAMIDIC CONE

"I was a technician salesman dealing in duplicating materials and servicing copiers," he said. "I'd reached my limit of progress there and realized the need for a change. Yet all the options open to me seemed equally dead-ended, or a demotion from the level I'd reached."

Inspired by the report he had read, Lew made himself a 12-inch cardboard cone and slipped it under his bed.

"Call me a cock-eyed optimist if you wish," he said, "and you could be right. The idea was to stir up my head and bring new ideas.

"It worked far better than I hoped. Not only did I get a new angle on my employment picture, but coincidences began going my way. Where before I'd had to plan and push, arranging each step in advance, laboring to make it come to pass, winning some and losing some, now I seemed to be swept up by a positive tide of events almost without volition."

A few weeks after he placed the cone in his bedroom, Lew met a girl at a disco. Her father was the owner of a real estate office.

"That was a line I had not much considered," Lew said. "I knew I needed to study for a real estate licence, but I'd never made any effort to find what else was involved or even what such work could pay."

His girlfriend was a mine of information. Her father was also helpful. In the shortest possible time Lew had his licence and entered real estate dealing.

"That brought me in contact with many influential people I would never have met as a technician," Lew said. "Keeping my eyes and ears open, I picked up invaluable data. Among other advantages, I invested on a broker's casual tips and prospered. I took the lead in commission earnings over my colleagues and thus received the 'plum' listings. Good fortune seemed to drop into my willing hands."

Lew soon quit real estate selling. His next step was to buy a ski resort. This was followed by ownership of a chain of motels.

"I sit back and let others work for me now," Lew an-

AMAZING NEW PSYCHIC PYRAMIDIC CONE 191

nounced. "I travel and keep an eye on my investments. That's when I'm not relaxing in my mountain chalet.

"Now the landing strip for my private plane is finished and the heated pool is constructed, I'm having a leisure mansion built above the snow line where I can take friends to enjoy nature. And the shape of that building is ... you guessed it! ... a 100-foot cone. If a little one can start such a sequence of delight, I'm wondering what a big one can do for my personal pleasure!"

MAKE A NEW PSYCHIC ENERGY CONE—OR JUST A "PRETEND" ONE: EQUALLY EFFECTIVE IN STARTLING RESULTS

A primary mystery about the Cone is that it does not have to be physically present in this mundane world to work its amazing effects.

By creating what occultists call a "thought form" in the shape of a cone, this "idea of a cone" has brought desired results for many people. Others have found they need to actually build a cone before it will work for them. The difference seems to depend on individual powers of mental visualization.

You can easily create a cone from a sheet of paper or thin card.

Draw a circle on it, any size. The larger the circle is, the larger your cone will be. But in this mysterious realm, *bigger* does not necessarily seem to be *better* or more powerful. Tiny cones created from two-inch circles have been proven devastatingly effective.

Standing a cup, bottle or can of beans on the paper and using that as a guide to draw around will make a very adequate sized circle.

Cut out the circle, and then cut a wedge-shaped piece

AMAZING NEW PSYCHIC PYRAMIDIC CONE

out of it, just like cutting a slice of pie. Cutting out a quarter of the "pie" will create a cone with a slope approximately equal to the slope of the Great Pyramid. The bigger the "slice" you cut from your circle, the more slim and pointed your cone will be.

Having cut out your slice, take the remaining portion of the circle and bend the two straight edges around to butt together. Secure them with a bit of tape and you have created your first *New Psychic Energy Cone.*

Creating a *mental* Cone as a thought form can be done in a multitude of ways. As I said before, that's an individual experience and methods vary widely.

If you habitually think in pictures in your mind, and "see" images inside your head when your eyes are closed, all you have to do is think about a cone, solid and three-dimensional, standing wherever you wish it to be. That works well for some.

Other people spend time mentally building a cone by making the first part of the *Digital Triad Gesture* (from Energy Circuit 7). They pretend that their moving finger tip is drawing a triangle of white light in the air. Then they imagine the triangle is turning on its axis, making a circle with the lower two points. The resulting mind shape is a glittering cone of white light which is then "thought" to be wafted into its operating position.

A further method is to "fix" the idea of the cone in your mind by looking steadily at a picture of a cone until, when you close your eyes, you can recall every detail as if it were truly in front of you. Most elementary art books carry pictures of cones, if you're seeking one to look at.

Whether you need a real cone or are able to use a mental one depends on many factors which are affected by your personal psychology and circumstances. For interest's sake, and because it can have such a magnificent effect on your life if you're one of the early users of Cone techniques, I urge you to experiment freely with this new concept.

AMAZING NEW PSYCHIC PYRAMIDIC CONE 193

RUTH W. IMAGINED NEW PSYCHIC ENERGY CONES AND GOOD FORTUNE ARRIVED

Having indicated to you how to create a mental *New Psychic Energy Cone,* this case history is the best example I know of such a routine being followed by interesting and beneficial results.

Ruth W. had been "on" to Pyramid Energy for about six months when she began experimenting with cones.

"I've always been a good visualizer and find it easy to place clear pictures of things on a kind of 'screen' in my mind," Ruth reports. "My use of cones consisted of making a mental picture of a cone of white light, imagining it to be situated wherever significant events could occur that could affect my life.

"If they'd been real cones, you'd have seen them all over the place! I "put" them in my boss' office, in the hospital ward with a sick relative, in my car, in the yard, on the roof of our home, and in class with my children.

"They were also mentally "planted" in places where a material cone could not easily be placed. I installed one in my husband's head, one in his boss' brain, and even one in my uterus.

"It was an experimental game. The idea was to bring the best influences to bear wherever I put a cone. I kept a written record of my thought form "placements" to keep track of any results.

"The number of apparent coincidences that followed are too numerous and precise, in my opinion, to be due to chance alone.

"My boss promoted me when few were being so favored; the relative was discharged from hospital a week earlier than anticipated; a patrol car flagged me down when I drove through a radar trap at double the legal limit—and I received only a caution when the police found their instruments reading incorrectly; the lettuces, tomatoes and grapes I

194   *AMAZING NEW PSYCHIC PYRAMIDIC CONE*

planted gave record yields; for the first time in years we lost no roof tiles in winter gales; my children's school grades improved.

"My husband, a designer, found an inspired solution to a long-standing engineering problem. His boss promptly made him head of his own department.

"And the cone inside me? We wanted another child, and I'd been having trouble conceiving. I'm happily pregnant now and the conception date seems to have been about 48 hours after I 'thought' a cone into my womb.

"I'm still experimenting, but that's my report to date. Backed by my written notes, wherever I placed a mental cone something good came up connected with it."

HOW TO VISUALIZE A 24-HOUR NEW PSYCHIC ENERGY CONE ANYWHERE

We've already looked at three ways to create a *New Psychic Energy Cone* with your mind. Having handled that, your task of putting the thought form where it will do most good is pure simplicity.

When you've decided where the Cone should be "put," all you need to do is to pretend it's there!

Close your eyes, recall the position the Cone needs to occupy and its surroundings, and you've got it.

If that seems too simple to be valid, you can make a temporary paper cone as previously instructed, place it where you wish your 24-hour *New Psychic Energy Cone* to have its effects, and sit gazing steadily at it for two minutes. Absorb the scene you're looking at so that any time later you can recall it from memory.

Having "fixed" that idea you can throw the paper cone in the trash—the mental image you can now call up will work just as effectively as the real thing.

AMAZING NEW PSYCHIC PYRAMIDIC CONE 195

"I'M CONVINCED MY NEW PSYCHIC ENERGY CONES HELPED CLEAN UP MY DEBTS," WRITES HANK G.

"Herewith a brief progress report on my personal experiments with Cone technology," writes Hank G. of Nebraska:

"January 1978: I was deeply in debt, for reasons I will not fully divulge. Suffice to say in 1977 I paid a considerable sum to the courts. My living expenses had taken second place (jail was the alternative if I failed to pay), so I had been living on credit. A medical expense not covered by insurance and a work lay-off (temporary) had creditors hounding me.

"February 1978: I re-entered regular employment, and made offers to all my creditors to pay them regular sums in proportion to my indebtedness to them.

"I began experimenting with Cones this month. I had a two-inch cone on my dining table; made a cone-shaped bill spike; kept a three-inch cone standing beside my telephone, on the north side; and another inside my mailbox. A fifth cone stood beside the front door, a sixth on my refrigerator, and a seventh under my bed at the head end on my side.

"April 1978: I was able to maintain all payments as and when due, which I frankly did not expect, having been overoptimistic in my earlier income estimates. I won $50 with a lottery ticket. Mr. A. mailed a check to me for $100 repayment plus interest of a three-year-old $75 loan I had written off as bad.

"May 1978: I won $1,000 by answering a simple question for a radio station when they called my number at random.

"June 1978: Last outstanding bill paid after receiving retroactive salary when my union negotiated a new contract.

"I make no claims of cause and effect, but I am convinced in my own mind that my *New Psychic Energy Cones* helped clear up my debts."

196   *AMAZING NEW PSYCHIC PYRAMIDIC CONE*

**YOUR NEW PSYCHIC ENERGY CONE HAS
UNLIMITED POWER FOR YOU TO USE**

Why do I call this concept a *New Psychic Energy Cone* instead of just a simple Cone? For the following reason: although the Cone has its own spectrum of healing and miracle-working powers, I see its use as a *part* of your *New Psychic Energy Power* tuning-in process.

If you were working purely with the power of the Cone, I would anticipate its acquiring another name to distinguish it from other metaphysical methods and energies.[1] But as an additional weapon in your armory of defenses against fate, I feel that your use of a Cone in the terms we are discussing is truly an extension of *New Psychic Energy Power.*

The specialized attributes of the Cone place healing high on the list. Printed reports I have on file attest to:

> Relief of pain by placing a Cone on the body of the sufferer.
>
> The disappearance of intestinal malfunctions by sitting with a Cone under the subject's chair.
>
> Rapid healing of broken bones.
>
> Improvement in retarded children.

Cone research is as open-ended as the Cone itself. I believe we have merely begun to discover the unlimited potential of an energy which may, in fact, supersede Pyramid Power, just as electricity and gas have made the wood-burning stove an obsolete anachronism.

Tap the power of a *New Psychic Energy Cone*—you could amaze yourself, and also become known as a pioneer in a new field of metaphysical research.

---

[1] Developing directly from the early and broad concepts presented exclusively to you in this Energy Circuit, the author is already involved in ongoing, state-of-the-art research into *Cosmic Conicology,* with a view to creating a self-help method using Cone power as the basic theme.

AMAZING NEW PSYCHIC PYRAMIDIC CONE **197**

"MIRACLES ARE MINE," STATES GLORIA M., NEW PSYCHIC ENERGY CONE USER

Gloria M. was the oldest user of Cone power known to me. She pooh-poohed the idea that this is a new concept.

"I'll be 93 in December this year," she said. "I was born in Spain in 1885 and I remember as a child my father putting paper cones over prime grapes to make them prize specimens. Did it to vegetables too.

"The old wise woman in our village had a black hat with a teeny brim all around. It came to a point making a cone on her noddle. She had signs sewn all over it and we kids were scared to death of her. They said she worked spells like nobody's business and would put the Evil Eye on any bad person for a few pesos.

"My husband used to make his watch keep time by stuffing it into a paper cone and standing it over a saucer. We've known about it in our family for centuries. My grandmother told me an ancestor of ours found treasure by working magic around a cone in a circle.

"But that's all ancient history, for you to believe or not as you like. I'm still using cones, and since they started writing books about it, I've been using cone energy properly and I tell you it works for me. Old ladies don't need much, but I make sure my pension check comes on time, the stove draws properly, the cats come in at night and I keep healthy, all by having cones around the house. Believe me, miracles are mine with those little pointy things.

"I'll make a prediction for you. When those UFO's finally land and make contact with all of us, we're going to find their saucers fly with cone energy, zipping through space quicker than the sun can run.

"I won't live to see that. I've had enough of this earth plane. I'll be leaving on the day after Christmas, and let cone energy take me to my Maker. I bet they know more about it on the Other Side than we do."

198 *AMAZING NEW PSYCHIC PYRAMIDIC CONE*

Gloria's second prediction came true. She died peacefully in her sleep on the evening of December 26, 1978. So perhaps we will find flying saucers use cone-concepts to energize their craft.

HOW, WHEN AND WHERE TO USE YOUR NEW PSYCHIC ENERGY CONE

As you will have realized, the field is wide open for experimentation in working miracles with your *New Psychic Energy Cone.*

I can indicate but a few of the amazing successes which have been achieved with the Cone, and repeat my encouragement to you to experiment.

Basically, you need to place your Cone at or near the center of the area which needs its destiny-changing powers.

Because a Cone can be created as a thought form, exciting vistas open up. You could not, for instance, place a *real* Cone in the mind of another person. But you *can* visualize a *mental* Cone inside the head of anyone—and users of such a technique vow that they have worked wonders of control, love and manipulation by making such a mind picture.

You may recall old humorous pictures of schoolrooms where the slow learner has been banished to a corner to wear a dunce cap. That custom of exposing the allegedly dull-witted to ridicule has now died out. But the fascinating feature of that old cap was that it was invariably cone-shaped!

We could wonder if the custom of placing a conical hat on a dullard's head was originally intended to focus the power of the Cone on his brain and thus stir up potential mental powers. Certainly the conical hat is prominently featured in legend as the headgear of astrologers, wizards and other magical workers!

AMAZING NEW PSYCHIC PYRAMIDIC CONE

So the practice of placing a real or imaginary cone over their heads is used by some people when they wish to get the words exactly right in a letter, or they wish to write a creative poem or find inspiration for a book. However, due to the overtones of the apparently ridiculous dunce cap, none of the Cone-wearers known to me will permit me to identify them.

I would advise you to try the *New Psychic Energy Cone* on any condition which needs change for the better. Use it in conjunction with any other techniques or methods; it almost inevitably increases the available energy.

I know a car owner in eastern Canada who places a thought form of a large Cone over his automobile when he parks it on the street every night. Despite being in an area notorious for vandalism, in four years he has never had his car broken into, no one has so much as scratched his fenders, and he swears his car starts easily on the iciest morning while his neighbors are fussing with booster cables, aerosol starter sprays, tow starts and other expensive and time-wasting assists to balky, cold engines.

Simply stated, placing a *New Psychic Energy Cone* thought form close to anyone or anything which needs to be changed for your benefit can produce satisfying and amazing results. I would be interested to hear of your experiments if you write to me c/o of this publisher. While I can not guarantee to reply to all letters (I receive too many to personally answer every one), I'll be delighted to hear of your research and results.

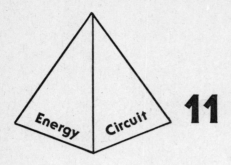

Creating Your Total New Psychic Pyramidic Environment

The succession of the preceding ten Energy Circuits has developed the idea of what *New Psychic Energy Power* can do for you, and has offered various methods of tuning in to the Cosmic Tides to bring you health, wealth and happiness.

Here we begin to take the separate elements of this method and tie them into a logical, organized structure designed to bring results easily, unerringly and with minimum fuss.

MAKING YOUR AKASHIC LIST OF DESIRES AND NEEDS

Probably one of the worst things that could happen to you would be to have your every last wish come true right now, like today. The overload of bounty would be just too much for you to handle. You can confirm that easily by checking up on what has happened to lottery winners who have received really big prizes. In the majority of cases the

YOUR NEW PSYCHIC PYRAMIDIC ENVIRONMENT   201

$1,000,000 winners are more disturbed and unhappy than they were before their big windfall.

That's neither old-fashioned Puritanism nor sour grapes talking to you. That's cold fact. Check on it if you wish. You'll have trouble contacting some of the big winners. Most of them are forced into hiding, while a high percentage commit suicide, unable to cope with the sudden life changes which much money brings.

So right up front I implore you to take it slow and easy with your potential miracles. Use *New Psychic Energy Power* to alter your life to glowing ecstasy one easy step at a time so you can adapt to the changes without turmoil. Luckily, that's exactly the way *New Psychic Energy Power* tends to work. As I've repeatedly told you, *New Psychic Energy Power* transforms things for your greatest good.

The first step to achieving this transformation is to make an *Akashic List of Desires and Needs*. And your initial decision requires you to distinguish between the similar, but very different, concepts of a need on the one hand and a desire on the other.

A *need* is something which has priority; it's something which *must* be acquired or attended to. Lack of attention to a need inevitably leads to trouble, strife and turmoil.

A *desire* is less pressing, even if some seem more urgent at the time they occur. A desire is a yearning for something it would be nice to own or have happen, but if it has to wait awhile you will not suffer anything worse than a mild frustration.

Having gotten those definitions behind us we can proceed. We're about to construct a working plan to create ideal conditions for you to get the most out of life. It's called your *Akashic List of Desires and Needs*.

Although you could do this next as a purely mental process, I suggest you'll lend more clarity and force to it if you write them down. So equip yourself with paper and pencil, and away we go.

202   YOUR NEW PSYCHIC PYRAMIDIC ENVIRONMENT

At the top, write "AKASHIC LIST, FIRST DRAFT." Now, as they come to mind, write down your desires and needs. All of them. Some will be material things, such as a new house, a new car, a private plane, a pool. Others will be abstract, such as good health, removal of frustration and the like. Others will concern relationships: a happy marriage, new and stimulating friends, a loving companion.

Let them all flow. Any lack or condition that needs changing for the better goes on your first draft.

Why are we doing this? It brings your problems out in the open, and shows which Cosmic Tides you need to attune with.

Have you written them all down? If so, begin on a fresh sheet of paper, heading it "AKASHIC LIST, SECOND DRAFT." Below that heading set up two columns, one headed "NEEDS" and the other "DESIRES."

In the light of the foregoing definitions, rewrite your list, putting the items under their appropriate headings. "$600 to pay back rent," would definitely qualify to be listed under "NEEDS." "A mink coat" is probably a desire—although "a new coat" would go under "NEEDS" if your old one is threadbare and winter is coming.

Even when you think your second draft is complete it's almost certain you've missed some items. Frequently our most pressing needs may not be obvious to us.

So apply a *New Psychic Energy Power* technique from Energy Circuit 8 to identify items for your list you may have overlooked, or may even have failed to realize need to go onto your Akashic List.

In Energy Circuit 8 you were told how to use your *Rhinal Energy Focus* while sleeping. Use the same method to update and complete your Akashic List.

Use your *Rhinal Energy Focus* as described, writing "What have I missed from my Akashic List?" on the pad which you put beside your bed with the technique. The rest of the routine is exactly as previously described in Energy Circuit 8.

YOUR NEW PSYCHIC PYRAMIDIC ENVIRONMENT 203

You'll be amazed in the morning to find you have not only identified previously unrecognized needs, but you may also have scribbled down quick solutions to existing ones!

Any new items which show up for your Akashic List should be added to it. And, of course, as soon as any needs or desires are satisfied, cross them off the list with a happy stroke of your pencil.

For very valid metaphysical reasons I suggest you carry out this *Rhinal Energy Focus* routine on alternate nights for a full month.

By the time the month has passed you'll have a comprehensive Akashic List, and you will naturally add or subtract from it during those weeks as your circumstances alter or further items occur to you.

As the weeks roll by, rewrite your Akashic List as you feel so inclined, heading it "THIRD DRAFT," "FOURTH DRAFT" and so on.

"MY AKASHIC LIST CAME TRUE LIKE ONE-TWO-THREE," WRITES RONALD D.

Pleasant to be able to record a total success. You could see Ronald D. as an A+ student of *New Psychic Energy Power,* and strive to emulate his example.

Apart from omitting his salutory introduction and close, the following is his letter in its entirety:

"You invited letters on how pyramid energy has worked for individuals. 'Very nicely, thank you' is my cheerful reply. I don't expect a reply to this letter as I know you're busy working, and I'm busy playing (for the first time in years) so I'll keep this as short as possible.

"My Akashic List was a long one. I needed everything from new shoes to a new personality, with a new body thrown in for good measure. I also needed a new (sexual reference deleted).

"I was poor, sick, weary, unloved, assailed by negative

204 YOUR NEW PSYCHIC PYRAMIDIC ENVIRONMENT

people and neurotic to the point of paranoia. Mind if we give that a miss? All in my past now, and I never again want mental pictures of the way I was in those abject days to defile my memory.

"I'd much rather indicate the peak I've reached in the 24 months since *New Psychic Energy Power* went to bat for me.

"I made the journey around the four faces of the *New Psychic Energy Generator.*

"My biggest need was money to get debt collectors off my back, my front porch, and my telephone. The North Face techniques brought me a girl with money coming out of her ears, in a succession of flukes a fiction writer wouldn't dare to use in a story. As well as getting cash, that also aligned with my East Face for a compatible lover. Not only rich, but also a sexual athlete, would you believe!

"With the 'heavies' gone to bug other debtors I hardly needed the South Face except to get even with a particularly aggressive collector who'd made my life a misery. He met up with a guy bigger than he is and took a free ride to hospital.

"The West Face routines put me back on my feet again, and with the North Face in forward drive hurrying goodies to me in a golden shower, I'm set for life.

"My Akashic List came true like one-two-three, although to be strictly accurate, I guess I should match that to the four faces of the pyramid and say it came true like one-two-three-four!"

WHICH TECHNIQUES TO USE FOR MOST BRILLIANT RESULTS

Energy Circuits 3 through 6 identified which faces of your *New Psychic Energy Generator* are connected with what elements of your life.

Following your Akashic List updating with the month of *Rhinal Energy Focus* work, run through the list and identify which desires and needs go with which face of your *New Psychic Energy Generator.*

YOUR NEW PSYCHIC PYRAMIDIC ENVIRONMENT   205

Mark each need or desire with its correct face name. It's easiest to use the initials "N," "E," "S" and "W" to identify north, east, south and west techniques respectively. Mark the appropriate initial against each item on your Akashic List. Put two or more initials against any item if you're in any doubt which category it falls under.

You now know which face techniques to apply to what problem as you move in on turning your *Akashic List of Desires and Needs* into sparkling satisfaction and total joy.

MARION S. "GOT IT RIGHT FIRST TIME" AND IS NOW A HAPPY MILLIONAIRE

Sure, I know I have said most people who win a million dollars are unhappy afterward. So Marion S. is one of the exceptions which prove the rule.

"I knew all about how big money upsets lives," Marion said. "I was prepared to take that chance. To walk into my bank and deposit a tax-free check for a million dollars was my abiding desire, yearning and craving. I saw myself doing it so hard, it hurt!"

Marion poured her heart and soul into trying to make her miracle come true, employing North Face routines on a daily basis.

"I devoured the *Golden Square of Prithivi* with my eyes," she said. "I *felt* that check in my fingers, *smelt* the ink as they piled crisp new $1,000 bills in front of me, *heard* the rustle of paper, *tasted* the celebration champagne, *saw* the printed 'PAY TO THE ORDER OF MARION S. ONE MILLION DOLLARS.' All in my mind of course, but I made it so real the excitement stayed with me when I was through with the routine each day."

The objective of this dedicated pyramid work was to win big with one of the five Canadian lottery tickets Marion had bought.

"I kept them beside the Golden Square on the table until

206   *YOUR NEW PSYCHIC PYRAMIDIC ENVIRONMENT*

the numbers were drawn," she relates. "I wanted to add every last quiver of energy to the process."

Marion could not take her eyes off the TV screen the night the draw was telecast.

"The first million-dollar number was nowhere near any of mine," she said. "So I just kept a picture of the Golden Square and the check in mind and waited."

The numbered balls were dropped into the random selection machine and the next number began.

"As they were read off from the left, they were *my* numbers," Marion recalls. "One of my tickets matched as the balls dropped. Only one gate was still flashing, which meant the ball had not yet fallen."

If that number was 3, Marion has won a million. If it was any other number from zero through 9, she would not win a thin dime.

"I remember whispering, 'Please God, let it be a three,' just as the last light stopped blinking," she said. "The girl stepped forward, took the last vital ball and held it up to the camera. At that precise instant my TV screen went on the blink. But by a miracle the sound continued."

The commentator strung out the suspense.

"And the last number, the one that makes all the difference ... the one we've been waiting for, the one which means some lucky person out there is a million dollars rich ... the final number is ... a three!"

Marion says she was suddenly very calm. She had become an instant millionaire.

"I thanked God, and then I thanked the Golden Square," she said, "although I see them as two faces of the same power. But Whoever or Whatever had granted me this boon, for once in my life I'd got it right the first time."

Marion experienced the joy of depositing her check, and has handled her fortune well. She bought a luxurious home and furnished it to her taste with about one-fifth of her windfall. The balance she has had invested in a trust fund which makes sure she will never need to earn another dime to

YOUR NEW PSYCHIC PYRAMIDIC ENVIRONMENT   207

keep her in opulence, and will benefit her children when they most need it.

"I knew what I was doing," she said. "In fact, when I won it was as though it was happening for the second time, so I felt no big trauma. My Golden Square rehearsals had prepared me in advance."

A QUICK TRIP TOGETHER AROUND THE FOUR FACES

To clarify and remind you of what has gone before, we can now take a quick look at the four faces of the pyramid.

The North Face is simple: material wealth and possessions are north's domain. No problem at all to decide which items on your Akashic List should have the letter "N" (for North) written against them reminding you to use the *Golden Square of Prithivi* to bring these things you can see and touch, such as hard cash and assets.

The East Face brings glory and joy for abstract needs. Love and Peace of Mind are the provinces of the east. You'll append the letter "E" to all emotional disturbances you wish dispelled with the help of the *Blue Circle of Vayu*.

Next to the South Face where you tune in to Protection and Offense. Read Energy Circuit 5 carefully before applying the magic of the *Scarlet Triangle of Tejas*—as noted, protection is often more peaceful than all-out war!

Finally, to the West Face to create abundant energy and total well-being for yourself, centered on the *Silver Crescent of Apas*.

KNOW YOUR DESTINY BY USING THE HORUS FUTURE TECHNIQUE

A part of your subconscious mind is able to travel up the time path into the future and bring back data which tells what's going to happen. J.W. Dunne conclusively proved that

208 *YOUR NEW PSYCHIC PYRAMIDIC ENVIRONMENT*

by statistical experimentation, and wrote about it in his book, *An Experiment with Time.*

However, unless you're a practicing psychic it's a definite challenge to get in touch with that part of your mind which can tell you tomorrow's events as clearly as a newspaper can tell you about yesterday's.

Herewith a technique which opens that door to your subconscious: the amazing *Horus Future Technique.*

What this method does is to instill in you the valuable ability known as "dreaming true." As you sleep, your future-knowing facility automatically feeds clear pictures into your mind, and they are experienced as dreams. When you wake in the morning, you find you retain clear and precise images of what's upcoming for you. With the addition of *New Psychic Energy Power* techniques, the information you receive is precisely tailored to ensure your growth, stability, security, happiness and well-being.

Knowing the future is excellent, but that's such a wide vista, you need to define a target or two.

So *you* decide what part of the future you wish to view, using methods already learned in this book.

If you wish to see what's going to happen moneywise, or what's the best move to make regarding a sale of an asset or the purchase of some material possession, you'll incorporate North Face influences.

If you wish to see how to achieve peace of mind, how it will come or who your lover will be, East Face influences are required.

Maybe you need to know who your enemies are, how to overcome them or what dangers you need to protect against. Using South Face methods will ensure such advance information being given to you.

Seeking your future health picture? Use West Face influences, and grow well and strong while avoiding any potential debilitating factors the future may hold.

Following the next case history, you'll be shown precisely how to apply this thrilling method of parting the mists of time to discover what destiny has in store for you. If you like the

YOUR NEW PSYCHIC PYRAMIDIC ENVIRONMENT **209**

picture presented, you can lie back and revel in it; if the
coming events are not to your satisfaction, you can simply
apply the correct *New Psychic Energy Power* technique and
evade the projected circumstances.

THE HORUS FUTURE TECHNIQUE SHOWED
HER WHAT NUMBERS TO PLAY

The slow clap of the security men rose above the hum of
voices and click of wheels and dice in the casino. Those in the
know straightened up and looked around them. The clapping
meant someone was winning, and not peanuts at that!

A telescope was unnecessary to detect the center of the
action. A girl was laying down chips on the roulette wheel
from a bigger pile of high denomination chips under her
trembling hands. At almost every spin the croupier pushed
more chips into her pile.

"I had a written list of numbers hidden in my hand,"
Abbie D., our lucky winner said. "All I had to do was follow
the list and place chips on those numbers. As soon as I won, I
went to the next number on the list.

"My scribbled note even told me what time to start
gambling. I went into the casino with $50 and came out with
$23,700. My first bet was $10 of my own money. That won
$350 on the first spin. After that I was able to play with the
casino's money, betting $100 a spin. I stopped when my
eighth and final number had come up."

No, Abbie was not in cahoots with the croupier. She had
not fixed the wheel. Neither had a dying gambler pressed the
numbers on her in gratitude for a last drink of water, as
happens in fiction.

Abbie had written those numbers herself, that morning.
She had gloriously proven the efficiency of the *Horus Future
Technique,* using the precise method described in the next
section.

"There's little to tell," Abbie said. "I was in Vegas, and
took my *New Psychic Energy Generator* along. Before I went

210   *YOUR NEW PSYCHIC PYRAMIDIC ENVIRONMENT*

to bed I looked at the Golden Square carrying the thought I would like to know about any winning numbers in my future.

"I woke with a picture of a digital clock at the front of my mind. I wrote down 4:00 p.m. and the date which it was showing and that brought a number to mind. As I scrawled it on my pad, seven more numbers came back to me out of my dreams. I scribbled them down also.

"I spent the day in happy anticipation, arriving at the table in time to make my first win, which spiraled into more money than I've ever seen in my life before."

HOW TO WORK THE HORUS FUTURE TECHNIQUE

The *Horus Future Technique* takes a few minutes of preparation just before you retire to bed.

First and foremost, make sure you have a paper and pencil handy when you wake; dreams have a habit of slipping away before you've finished your first cup of coffee. You need to make your first morning move that of picking up your pad and recording the highlights of the night's dreams.

But that's jumping the gun. We have yet to "trigger" those dreams correctly.

Decide what you wish to know about your future, and which face of the pyramid applies to the area you wish to examine. Having decided, sit down and view the appropriate symbol on your *New Psychic Energy Generator* for two minutes. Whether you're looking at the gold, blue, scarlet or silver symbol, try to impress it on your mind.

When the two minutes are up, climb into bed, turn out the light (or darken the room if you sleep during the day), and close your eyes. Recall the symbol you've been gazing at. Remember its shape and color.

Begin counting slowly, in your mind, from one to whatever total you reach as you drift into sleep.

As you realize you're waking up in the morning, reach for your pencil and while holding in your mind *the very first thing*

YOUR NEW PSYCHIC PYRAMIDIC ENVIRONMENT 211

you thought of as you were coming to consciousness, write down your dream or dreams.

Holding to that "first thought" as you start to write will trigger your mind into handing you your dream, even if you're a person who has often said "I *never* dream."

The clarity and accuracy of this news of the future can amaze you. However, note the advice which follows the next case history if you wish your future knowing to achieve maximum potential and value.

TOM A. WAS "NOWHERE" A YEAR AGO: NOW HE'S "ON TOP OF THE HEAP"

"It was a dream that brought me from nowhere a year ago and put me on top of the heap," plutocrat Tom A. said. "I sometimes wonder if this is still a dream, and have to pinch myself to be sure I'm awake."

He was recording those words for this book in a Lear jet, cruising smoothly high above the sparkling sea. The sun glittered on his huge diamond stickpin and emerald ring as he accepted a rare brandy from his personal valet.

"I'm on my way to my private island," he said, "having gotten a mite bored with the jetset whoop-de-do in San Francisco. I dropped by to see the books at my electronics plant before I departed. Another five million for me—sometimes I wonder what to do with all the cash rolling in."

Scant months before, Tom had been down and almost out. His artisan job with a milling company had folded and his future looked bleak.

"The employment people offered me a hog-farming job up north, sweeping a National Monument in California, or janitoring in Chicago," Tom recorded. "They all sounded like a drag, but a bit better than food stamps. Yet which one was I to choose?"

A new leisure interest for Tom was Pyramid Energy, although he had merely trifled with it, not anticipating it would be of any help.

212   *YOUR NEW PSYCHIC PYRAMIDIC ENVIRONMENT*

"I'd recently come across the *Horus Future Technique* and this seemed a good time to give it a work-out," Tom said. "I had trouble deciding which face to view, so I did it by elimination. Health and strength it wasn't, so the West Face I could forget. Protection? I decided not, so now it was between the East and North Faces.

"I finally settled for the East Face, debating before I viewed the Blue Circle what would bring me most peace of mind. I counted and dropped asleep."

Tom says he has no recall of writing on his paper next morning, but when he was fully awake the written words jogged his memory.

"Until I read the paper I was quite sure I had not dreamed," he said. "But seeing 'Pig, Beard, Mansion, Money' barely legible on the sheet brought back a fleeting glimpse of a dream of a bearded man giving me a wad of bills to bed down some pigs in an oceanfront property."

Tom figured that meant he should go farming with the grunters.

"Wowie! The *Horus Future Technique* was right, even if I'd only got part of it and garbled at that," he said. "The owner of the pig farm, a bearded old guy by the way, was rolling in dough. A week after I started with him as hogsitter he decided to give it all up, sell the herd, and move to warmer climes.

"He kept me on in a new position he called 'Entertainment Admiral,' whistled up his private cruiser and off we sailed to the Bahamas. All I had to do was draw on a bottomless expense account to arrange parties and other diversions. The old boy was paying me so much I was able to hire a guy to work for me! All I did was say, "Friday we'll be in Georgetown so let's make that orgy-town' and it was fixed.

"That went on for half a year, then the old guy said he was going to retire me on a pension for meritorious service. Said he'd see me all right, and it was tax deductible anyway. He threw a fabulous farewell party for me, but didn't say a word about the pension.

YOUR NEW PSYCHIC PYRAMIDIC ENVIRONMENT   213

"As I was packing to leave the next day, with a kingsize hangover, a servant brought me an envelope. Inside were the deeds to a superb waterfront property in Los Angeles, all expenses paid for 20 years, and a legal contract making me sole owner of a thriving semiconductor manufacturing plant.

"When I went to thank him, I found the old boy had flown to Australia to see a girlfriend for the weekend."

Tom was fixed for life. Now he emulates his benefactor. Occasionally they meet and exchange experiences over a mint julep.

"I once asked him why he did all that for me when he'd known me only as an employee for a few months," Tom said. "The old guy harrumphed and hawed, and actually blushed. I squeezed it out of him in the end.

"Seems he'd had my baggage searched when I first arrived just in case I was a thug planning to knock him off and steal his cash. He copied the *Horus Future Technique* because he didn't understand it at first glance. Then he tried it out and that started us on the move to the Bahamas. He used the technique regularly and guided his investments and future path even more successfully.

"His gesture to me was merely a big fat thank-you, even if I didn't know why at the time."

POINTS TO WATCH TO REFINE YOUR NEW PSYCHIC ENERGY POWER

Briefly, I have one word for you to ensure unbelievable success with your *New Psychic Energy Power.* That word is: PRACTICE!

You're opening up paths in your mind which have never before felt the quiver of neurons. Your whole mind, body and soul is harmonizing with Cosmic Energies which you may have been battling against for years.

So although some readers will instantly see ecstatic

214   YOUR NEW PSYCHIC PYRAMIDIC ENVIRONMENT

results, others will need to run the techniques a number of times to get their metaphysical muscles in trim.

Your conscious mind can also be an inhibiting factor which slows down results: strong prejudices or early conditioning can mean you'll take longer than average to accept the incredible benefits which accrue from tuning in to the Cosmic Tides.

The life-shaping energy fields of destiny are all around you. The techniques for aligning with them are in this book.

The only other factor in the equation is *you*. *Apply* the techniques. Then instead of fighting a losing battle against the Cosmos you most assuredly will see the truly fantastic consequences of harmonizing with the energies of destiny which can carry you to supreme happiness and contentment.

An important thought fits well right here. When working any of the methods described in these pages, do not struggle and strain to get results. A relaxed mind and body is far easier for the Tides to manipulate for greatest effect.

So if you're habitually tense and nervous, you could consider starting a routine of lying down and telling yourself to relax for a few minutes a day, every day.

Some people will actually feel guilty about such apparent "escapism." Lying down and deliberately trying to think of nothing and letting strains and stresses flow out of their bodies is seen as a waste of valuable time.

Believe me, it's not a waste of anything! As you lie down and relax, tell yourself it's O.K. to ignore your problems for a little while. Sure, you'll attend to anything that needs doing when you've finished relaxing, but just for ten minutes or so make your priority that of unwinding and letting yourself ride with Cosmic Tides.

No need to take my word for it. Try it, regularly, for a couple of weeks. You'll be the first to witness the incredible benefits.

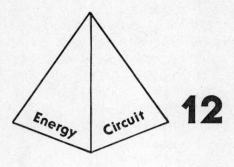

Journey to the Apex for a Lifetime of Miracles

To fully explain the theme of this Energy Circuit, I would have to write another complete book. One day I shall do that, where we explore metaphysical realms known as the etheric, the astral and the causal planes.

We would discover the concepts which have prompted latter-day scientists to suggest that this universe resembles nothing so much as a Cosmic Thought in the mind of God. We would gain an inkling of the total 'one-ness' of this existence, where we exist as a shimmering energy pattern forming a necessary part of a greater energy pattern.

Above all we would realize that you are much more than a physical body with a brain and mind. We would find that you have your existence as a person and individual in unimaginable planes of existence, and that your physical presence is only a tiny part of your total being which stretches from here to the stars and far beyond, from the forgotten past into the infinite future, and into other planes of awareness partly explored by dedicated mystics.

216   *JOURNEY TO THE APEX*

So you will find mystery in this final Energy Circuit. Some mystery because space does not permit full explanation, and because such explanation is superfluous to the purpose of this particular book. But more mystery because the human mind is not yet equipped to grasp the concepts and put them into words on a printed page.

We are going to take a journey together, and the purpose of that journey revolves around two metaphysical maxims. The first states: "Once the preparations have been properly made, the result is already a fact."

The second states: "Anything performed in the Astral Plane will assuredly become physical reality when time has wrought its magic on the Astral formation."

I state those for information only. If you understand those maxims, all well and good. If they are part of the mystery of this Energy Circuit as far as you are concerned, have no worries: by following me along a mental path, guided by my words, you will achieve results. There is no more need for you to understand the precise "why" of it, than there is for you to be an engineer and fully understand why your car works before you drive it!

This journey takes place purely in your mind. You are going to aid your attunement with the Tides by setting up and preparing conditions in the Astral Plane.

THE JOURNEY TOGETHER SO FAR

Before you take any journey, certain preparations have to be made.

Whether it's a familiar vacation trip or an expedition to the Brazilian interior, you have to pack clothes, arrange for accommodation of some sort, check your transport, confirm your provisions and similar chores.

All the 11 foregoing Energy Circuits partly represent such preparations. Even though they have incredibly wonderful side effects in the shape of bringing your wishes into reality, the exercises and techniques so far described have

JOURNEY TO THE APEX

217

been carefully designed to prepare your mind, body and soul to take a guided tour of the *Astral City of New Psychic Energy Power.*

THE ASTRAL CITY OF NEW PSYCHIC ENERGY POWER

You will not find the *Astral City of New Psychic Energy Power* marked on any map. No registered Travel Agent will sell you a package tour of that wonderful place.

Yet the Astral City exists. But not in the material plane, on the surface of the Earth. Nor in, under or above this Earth, either—leastwise, not any distance you can measure with a steel tape and theodolite. And we're not about to travel to the stars and planets in search of this elusive Astral City.

As its name implies, the *Astral City of New Psychic Energy Power* exists on the Astral Plane, a realm which is close by. And the door for your awareness, the real You, to pass through to reach the Astral City is within your own mind.

You've visited the Astral City many times, in sleep. Your awareness regularly roams its tree-lined avenues and green parks.

Part of what I'm going to do is tell you more about the Astral City, so your memory is tweaked. Then some time in the future, while your physical body lies deeply sleeping, your dreaming self will not only visit the Astral City but will also bring back some of the ineffable peace and incredibly glorious feelings of fulfillment, so they carry over into your waking life.

"VISITING" THE ASTRAL CITY TURNED LIFE AROUND FOR SCOTT B.

"I am not much a word person. Actions always spoke louder than words to me," attests Scott B. "As requested, I

JOURNEY TO THE APEX

will try to tell how my involvement with the Astral City turned my life around."

Scott is a long-time acquaintance of mine. We first encountered each other at a seminar I was holding on astral travel in 1973. Part of the induction consists of a journey to the Astral City, taken in a group. After the experience, individuals are invited to keep in touch to relate what experiences transpired.

"On Monday morning, that is two days after the group session at the seminar, I awoke feeling invigorated and refreshed, anxious to be up and doing," Scott wrote. "Unusual for me—I have always been a 'Blue Monday' type.

"I kept a specially vivid dream of the Astral City. I seemed to have met a guardian angel or some such entity. If you recall, at the seminar I had placed the idea of escaping from the ratrace as my major goal in life."

Scott's narrative continues by witnessing the fact that he was much more relaxed and peaceful than usual. His week at work went with less stress.

"I was a metal-press operator," he said. "Usually by the weekend the noise and hassles had me sniping at my workmates, threatening to beat up on my wife, and spending Saturday unwinding with a crate of beer.

"Each night during that unusual week I dreamed I was drawing closer to a source of harmony and light, and this is where words to describe it fail me. On the Saturday of that week I hopped out of bed like a teenager, singing and whistling, on top of the world. My wife found it most unexpected."

Scott found he was anxious to be on the move. By 9:00 a.m. he was driving his rec vehicle down the highway.

"I was laughing and joking," Scott said. "My wife and kids, riding with me, were stunned. It was the first Saturday in five years I had not crawled out of bed at noon, wolfed a bite to eat, then vanished unshaven and unapproachable into the den, popped a can of beer and turned on the TV, emerging snarling for more food at sundown.

JOURNEY TO THE APEX **219**

"We arrived at the lake and got set up for a little fishing, relaxing and play."

Thus the curtain went up on a new phase of life for Scott.

"We met a painter that weekend, and visited his art studio in the hills," Scott said. "We became close friends, and both my wife and I took up landscape painting. That was a laugh: I didn't dare tell my colleagues for a long while—I thought those jocks would say I was losing my masculinity. Yes, I was *that* macho!

"I became a competent artist. Not Renoir or Constable, but steadily selling my work. Soon we were making more at spare-time painting than I was pulling down at the bench. Upshot was I quit and painted fulltime. We bought a big old house on a couple of acres with a mountain view and made it our studio and home.

"Just as I'd announced as a target at the seminar, I had left the ratrace behind. I'm my own boss now, working as and when I please, with no pressure, no problems. Not rich, but comfortable and always enough for immediate needs. My family relationships have improved out of all recognition, and I have a peaceful knowledge inside of me that's the way it's going to be from now on.

"My next project is to paint a picture of the Astral City the way it seems to me. I shall try to bring out the serenity and security of that holy place, as a testimony to the new life I've found from it."

EXPLORE THE ASTRAL CITY WITHOUT LIFTING A FINGER

Your first fully recalled journeys to the *Astral City of New Psychic Energy Power* will take place while you sleep. You will awaken to recall the City as an especially vivid dream. A dream so sharp and real, carrying such overtones of quietude and security, you'll never feel harassed, threatened or insecure again.

220 *JOURNEY TO THE APEX*

You'll begin to enter that incredibly *peaceful* life of the Adept where the *true* meaning of Jesus' words, "Take therefore no thought for the morrow: for the morrow shall take thought for the things of itself," becomes part of your life.

Later you'll be able to sit quietly in a chair in your leisure time and move your awareness to the Astral City without going to sleep.

Here I will give you an outline of the journey you take in your mind. As you practice this, the Astral sleeping experience will fill in the details until the Astral City becomes as familiar to you as your own home town.

Read the following words slowly, stopping at frequent intervals to close your eyes and think about what I am describing.

"We are standing together on an open windswept plain or prairie, with low rolling hills in the distance.

"A broad, straight gravel road leads through the grass and scrub to the hills. We walk forward along the road, and the hills come closer.

"The road slopes upward and we approach the summit, and as we pass over the crest of the hill we see a green, lush valley before us.

"And on a hill on the other side of the valley towers a great gray stone wall, surrounding a city. That is the *Astral City of New Psychic Energy Power.*

"We can see a great iron-studded wooden gate in the wall as we approach after crossing the valley. Sentries pace the walls above.

"We arrive together at the base of the wall to find rough stonework pillars on either side of the great gate. Above, a sentry calls, asking our business.

"Reply: 'We are seekers who have come to the gates of the Astral City. In the Name of Those who built this City, and in the Name of Him who built Them, open the gates.'

"The mighty gates swing back, showing us the Astral City within the walls, bathed in sunlight.

"A broad avenue flanked by graceful trees leads straight

JOURNEY TO THE APEX

from the gate toward a flat-topped pyramid in the center of the City.

"We walk out of the shadow of the gate along the avenue. We reach the base of the pyramid which now towers above us. It is built in steps which we begin to mount.

"The going is easy as we climb the 32 steps which lead to the flat top of the pyramid. As our eyes come level with the top step we see a massive white marble Hall in the center of the top.

"We reach the top step and walk toward the Hall across a marble forecourt, smoothed by the feet of multitudes who have taken this journey before us.

"We step inside the Hall, to see a vaulted roof high above us. In the center of the echoing Hall is a double cube of stone.

"We stand before the smooth white double cube of stone in the center of the Hall. The two cubes stand side by side, each three feet high.

"A shaft of pure white light descends from above and illuminates you. As you stand in this glorious spotlight, think about your *Akashic List of Desires and Needs.* Consider your main goal in life. What do you wish to be? What do you wish to have? Where do you wish to be?

"Think about achieving your goal. Enjoy it, as if it had already happened. Experience it. Be *in* it. Live it in your mind.

"In this Astral Place your goal is created.

"And it is now time to leave the Hall—but you will encounter this place many times again. Now that you know the way you will return.

"Turn and walk out to the brightness and down the steps, seeing the Astral City spread out below you. Walk the avenue to the gate which admitted us. As the gate swings open pass through and walk down the hill toward a river which crosses the valley below.

"We find a graceful boat moored to the bank. We step aboard and the boat drifts out on the waters, moving with the currents and tides.

"You are returning to the real world, the here and now."

222   *JOURNEY TO THE APEX*

Read that foregoing passage to yourself before retiring on any night you are not doing *Rhinal Energy Focus* work on your Akashic List (as described in Energy Circuit 11).

PEGGY R. LEARNED SECRET NEWS IN THE ASTRAL CITY

Something mysteriously disturbing was going on in Peggy R.'s life. She had an ominous dread of the future. Intuitively she felt her security was threatened by coming events.

"Nothing I could describe in words," she said, "but it was making me irritable and jumpy. I was wound up like a bowstring, snapping at my husband and cutting the kids off at the knees.

"My previously acceptable, if unexciting, marriage started to fray at the seams. If I didn't get my head straight soon we were heading for a separation. I tried to throw it off but the cloud of pending doom grew thicker.

"I fought to relax, looking for leisure involvements to take my mind off this hovering menace. I was starting to wonder if I'd been bewitched."

That train of thought led Peggy to psychic and metaphysical books, especially as she found reading helped her to ignore the feelings of calamity which haunted her.

"The library books offered me plenty of possibilities of what could be going on, some of them scary. Yet I found no firm direction on how to get out from under this sensation. That was before I read about the Astral City."

Sitting quietly, musing about the concept of the Astral City she had just read, Peggy drifted into a reverie.

"I knew perfectly well I was sitting in the good chair in the living room, with the kids yelling in the yard and my husband watching TV in the rec room. Yet my attention—my awareness, I guess you would call it—was in the Astral City.

"I saw the Hall, and stood on the pyramid. And on a smooth marble wall before me, something like a movie

JOURNEY TO THE APEX

flickered into being. I was looking down on our house, as if from a helicopter, and dust was billowing up all around it. Bulldozers and diggers were wrecking the whole area. Behind the destruction crept other machines, burrowing through the ground.

"The scene shifted to a small village some ten miles from our home. It too was being rebuilt, but where the wrecking around our home had been ominous and threatening, the expansion of the village seemed happy and ongoing. Just before the vision faded I saw an airy, contemporary structure rising, surrounded by new town houses and separate homes. I somehow knew I was seeing a haven of peace for us all. Then I found myself firmly back in the living room."

Thus began a relocation for Peggy and her family.

"I discussed the whole picture with my husband," Peggy said. "Probably to keep me quiet he took me to see some real estate in that village I'd seen in my vision. Prices were real low in that backwater."

Within six months Peggy and her family were installed in a beautiful home on a bluff overlooking the river which meandered through the village.

"We sold our old house for an excellent price and my husband found new work within walking distance of home, where previously he had commuted 80 miles each day," Peggy related. "The feelings of doom receded, yet I was still puzzled about the vision. Had it all been symbolic of destroying an old life and rebuilding afresh?"

It was more than that. Within a year, plans for a rapid transit system were passed in the city. A spur line was approved to run underground and surface at the village where Peggy had relocated.

"Just as I saw it so long before, our old house and the surroundings were bulldozed into rubble. Property prices fell drastically there. If we'd stayed we'd have gotten only a fraction of our home's value when it was taken over," Peggy said. "On the other hand our village grew to modern maturity with the influx of dormitory workers using the new subway.

224　　　　　　　　　　　　　　*JOURNEY TO THE APEX*

"We had bought an unused lot for a song in the village soon after we moved there. I had persuaded my husband it was an investment. The final proof of my vision fell into place soon after.

"On that lot has risen the office and apartment complex I saw. The developers bought our lot for an incredible price, and our new home has doubled in value.

"The secret news I received in the Astral City certainly paid off for us in the material world."

CREATING LIFE MIRACLES BY VISITING THE ASTRAL CITY

When you reach the flat top of the pyramid in the *Astral City of New Psychic Energy Power,* and enter the white marble hall, you know two things.

First, that you're harmonized with all four of the Cosmic Tides, and can expect to see frustrations and obstacles dissolving like butter on a hot bun.

Second, you've reached a powerful state of mind where whatever you picture with your brain will assuredly become reality and fact, *provided you're able to handle the consequences of what you're visualizing.*

Those last few words reinforce the concept of *New Psychic Energy Power.* The surging Tides of the Cosmos are on your side: their purpose is to carry you to well-being if you'll float along with them. If unsuspected obstacles can come from the fulfillment of a need or desire you demand to be met, the Tides will wait until the time is right and you're ready to gain greatest harmony from that happening.

This is why we hear William Cowper's words often quoted: "God moves in a mysterious way, His wonders to perform." Destiny (which you can consider as the manifestation of the Prime Mover's Will) may take you to happiness by a different route from the one your logic seems to indicate.

So if you're demanding a miracle and it fails to materialize, know that the Cosmic Tides are telling you something.

JOURNEY TO THE APEX 225

They're suggesting that you're aiming incorrectly, and happiness will come to you from a different direction—one you may least expect, after life events which you were unaware were coming.

Note in the next case history how Mike reached success in a totally unexpected manner.

ALSO-RAN MIKE H. IS A BIG WINNER TODAY

"I always thought the way to material wealth and comfort was to have a multiple bet come up at the track, or failing that, to be left a fortune by a rich aunt," Mike H. said. "If I ever had any rich relatives I never heard about them, and my luck on the horses was lousy. But that didn't stop me from trying to get wealthy from gambling."

Mike cannot recall how Pyramid Energy came into his life. He thinks he heard about it from a friend. Its chief attraction for Mike was that it apparently promised vast riches.

"So my mind picture was of me in a sharp suit with a roll of bills thick as your wrist in my pocket," he said. "I'd see myself lining up to collect winning bets, to the envy of the losers.

"But that picture stayed in my mind. At the track I continued to tear up my losing tickets as my selections finished out of the money."

Later Mike was able to smile at how his mental picture dropped into focus in a different way.

"I'd been laid off from my construction job," Mike related. "At the unemployment center I heard something new was in town. An outfit from Burbank was shooting a movie and was hiring extras like crazy."

Mike gladly took the temporary job and spent a week in work which was totally new to him.

"I enjoyed it hugely," he said, "and I also enjoyed the pay. On the third day they needed someone to walk on in a

226   *JOURNEY TO THE APEX*

bar scene and be roughed up. The casting director picked me out, saying I was a natural for the part. Wardrobe tricked me out to look like a city gent, and I did my bit."

At the end of the day's shooting, Mike, still in costume, had just collected his pay, when the director buttonholed him.

"He said the producer liked my style in the bar scene, and was I interested in a bigger part? I jumped at the chance," Mike recalls, "and some of the guys I'd met on the set congratulated me, although I could see they wished they'd got the part instead of yours truly."

That exposure was Mike's step into riches. He does regular TV and movie work now, and his agent finds him in steady demand.

"John Travolta I'm not," Mike said, "but I'm making a fantastic living about ten times better than in construction.

"Took me months to see how Pyramid Energy had put it together. The sharp suit, the money, the envy of the losers—it was all there, only it wasn't at the track. It was on a movie set, and that's somewhere I'd never imagined myself. Pyramid Energy, you're a great friend to come home to!"

NEW PSYCHIC ENERGY POWER COMBINES PERFECTLY WITH YOUR RELIGION AND PHILOSOPHIES

Several times so far I have mentioned your Creator, God, the Prime Mover, and other titles attributed to the Great Architect who designed this fabulous universe we inhabit.

Yet some of you will nurse doubts, simply because some of the concepts offered are not those you will find in your average Sunday school class. Thus I know if I omit the following, I will receive sacks of letters asking me if this method of making life peaceful and full is connected with pagan worship, "forbidden" knowledge or worse.

Whatever your religion, the promise it offers is ultimate peace and glory. You may see your God as a benevolent bearded patriarch, or as an Omnipotent One too glorious to

JOURNEY TO THE APEX

be approached except through His emissaries, or your God may even be pantheistic, evident only in the miraculous way this whole Cosmos operates.

Whatever your beliefs, the energies and powers we have been investigating are truly part of your Creator's plan, and they are provided to carry you to happiness if you'll allow them to.

That's the basic credo of this book. No matter what religion you adhere to, nothing I have suggested you do is in conflict with any theological understandings of which I am aware.

That clear-cut and unequivocal guarantee should reassure anyone who is even faintly worried about the new realms of the mind we are exploring here.

TERRI L. TELLS HER SUCCESS STORY IN HER OWN WORDS

I will not attempt to paraphrase Terri L.'s own words. Share her joy as she allegorically relates how Pyramid Energy swept her to sublime happiness.

"I suppose, like Alice, I should begin at the beginning, go on to the end and then stop. Except there never was a beginning I can recall, and the end is not yet—with each day bringing greater delights and wonders. Words are but blunt tools to sculpt an epitaph on the blank catacombs of the past.

"I labored each day in a dark prison. A prison not so much of the body but of the mind. Pain, cold and grief were my companions; hunger and poverty my oppressors. My heart beat unwillingly, awaiting a release that never came.

"Each dawn was the gray herald of dull tragedy, another rusting nail in a coffin of sorrow and hopelessness. The sun might shine on others, but I was the outcast in the shadows.

"I fought. God, how I fought! To the limits of my aching body, my fevered brow, my failing spirit, I strove to raise myself from the pit of black ugliness where the touch of a

JOURNEY TO THE APEX

friendly hand would have been heaven, and a kindly word a rapture beyond price.

"No hand moved in the darkness, except to take, and beat, invade, and exit. No mouth formed words to aid me in my agony. Dull and mindless, I felt that destiny lay on my soul like a rotting corpse, eyeless and reeking, pressing me deeper into the slimy depths.

"Yet did I see a light in that timeless place. A small brave light. Who dared illumine that dank dungeon of depravity?

"My chains, my bonds ... they tremble, fray and fall! A tremulous flame of hope stirs in my breast, reflecting the greater glory shining on the path ahead. Move, failing limbs. Draw on the Power. Begone, ye bats of blackness!

"I walk, gaining strength. Toward the Light. A great door reverberates sullenly in the night of terror behind me. I am bedazzled ... clean ... free!

"Sweet as nectar flow the tears of joy. Protective are the arms around me. Strangers greet me, strangers named warmth, comfort and peace. Strangers no more, for they are with me to eternity.

"You will excuse me, please, for my Prince cometh. We go together to the Hall in our benison of love, to bathe in wealth beyond imagery. Riches to feed the body; riches to expand the mind; riches to weave a symphony to which my soul sings.

"Dawn brings myriad delights, new days a tranquil knowing of harmony. And the night, a gentle swinging of time's pendulum, brings repose to prepare again for the coming of the Light which ever shines."

Terri's words, mystic and obscure for some, describe her transformation from disease-ravaged prostitute to volunteer worker at a spiritual retreat in Canada, after encountering Pyramid Energy concepts.

She hopes others will gain such inspiration, and reach those sublime heights where the meanings and truths underlying her words can be fully understood.

JOURNEY TO THE APEX

REACH OUT FOR IT AND NEW PSYCHIC ENERGY POWER WILL BRING IT TO YOU

Sincere thanks to you for staying with me throughout these pages. Your time and efforts are appreciated, not only by myself, the author of this book, but more importantly by the Cosmic Tides that shape your destiny.

The first results of your application are already shaping up in the unseen planes. Your Akashic List is a fact. Your needs and desires are recorded, both on paper and in your future. Perhaps for the very first time in your life, you're learning to let Cosmic Tides carry you along to glory, to see your life turned around to happiness the like of which you have never considered in your most wishful fantasies.

What has been our objective throughout these pages?

In summary, we have proposed that any lack or discomfort in your life is due to your unwitting or deliberate misalignment with the Creative Tides of this incredible universe.

Then we have learned simple techniques by means of which to swim *with* those Tides so you are effortlessly provided with all the things you have been missing for so long.

Enjoy your future, and may the Cosmic Energies bring you the feeling of harmony, peace and happiness which is not only your birthright, but is the way the Great Architect intended life to be.

New Psychic Energy Power is yours, to revel in, to soak away your cares and pains and replace them with peace, tranquility and all the perfection of this Cosmos.

Swim in the tides, relax and float to your ecstatic destiny as the harmony of the Cosmic Spheres invites you to. If you prefer the phrase, "Let go and let God."

We will meet in the Astral City, you and I, in the Hall. May you soon acquire clear memories of those meetings, and others far more transcendental. Until then, farewell.